Please check all items for damages
before leaving the Library.
Thereafter you will be held
responsible for all injuries
to items beyond reasonable wear.

7-15 ④
8-16 6

Helen M. Plum Memorial Library

Lombard, Illinois

A daily fine will be charged for
overdue materials.

OCT   2013

MAKE
DIFFICULT
PEOPLE
DISAPPEAR

~ A Workplace Fable ~

How to Deal with Stressful Behavior and Eliminate Conflict

MONICA WOFFORD

WILEY

John Wiley & Sons, Inc.

Published by John Wiley & Sons, Inc., Hoboken, New Jersey.
Published simultaneously in Canada.

For general information on our other products and services or for technical support, please contact our Customer Care Department within the United States at (800) 762-2974, outside the United States at (317) 572-3993 or fax (317) 572-4002.

Wiley publishes in a variety of print and electronic formats and by print-on-demand. Some material included with standard print versions of this book may not be included in e-books or in print-on-demand. If this book refers to media such as a CD or DVD that is not included in the version you purchased, you may download this material at http://booksupport.wiley.com. For more information about Wiley products, visit www.wiley.com.

Library of Congress Cataloging-in-Publication Data:

Wofford, Monica, 1971-
    Make difficult people disappear : how to deal with stressful behavior and eliminate conflict / Monica Wofford.
       p.   cm.
    ISBN: 978-1-118-27380-7 (cloth); ISBN: 978-1-118-28363-9 (ebk);
    ISBN: 978-1-118-28457-5 (ebk); ISBN: 978-1-118-28732-3 (ebk)
    1. Problem employees.   2. Supervision of employees.   3. Stress management.
    I. Title.
    HF5549.5.E42W645   2012
    650.1'3—dc23

                                                                                    2011050800

Printed in the United States of America

10 9 8 7 6 5 4 3 2

Contents

Acknowledgments

After reading a book titled *Make Difficult People Disappear*, you might surmise that there's a great many difficult people in my world to thank for the inspiration. Quite the opposite is true. While the author of any book puts the actual pen to paper, it is always the multitude of friends, family, colleagues, clients and even strangers who influence the content. Life always provides the lessons that we can't begin to fabricate without our shared experiences and the wisdom gained from those times of triumph and turmoil.

There are many to thank for the examples they've provided, experiences they've enhanced, and guidance they so graciously added to this work. Although only a few are mentioned by name, many others of you know who you are. First and foremost, gratitude goes to those I might call my cheering section. They are the ones who noticed when I was being difficult and loved me or cheered me on anyway. Consistent doses of friendship and guidance were shared by Ron Karr, Terry Brock, Matt Holt, Imad Raad, Jeffrey Gitomer, Christine O'Neil, Sabrina VanNess, Claire Evans, and Kathy Potts. Each team member at Hudson Booksellers and John Wiley & Sons, especially my talented and kind editors, Adrianna Johnson and her partner in crime Susan Moran, have provided unending guidance and thought-provoking feedback that always seemed to land in a way that conveyed respect and caused me to strive to be better. All of my training and coaching clients have inspired me to learn as much from them as perhaps they have from me—whether you have appeared on CSPAN, been president of a major theme park, run your own business, influenced the entire labor movement, led a nonprofit, sold insurance, actively led the "Got Milk?" campaign, controlled national air travel, measured the nation's standards, provided pest control, or influenced every major software launch the world has ever seen. Each audience member and Contagious Conference participant has given me feedback that what we share makes a difference. Each family member has inspired me to better understand myself and others—whether you have shared the humor of the Dr. Suess story I read at your wedding, reminded me of the difference between difficult and different, or given me reason to develop my own strength. The co-creators of the CORE® Profile, Dr. Sherry Buffington and Gina Morgan, have become like an adopted Mom and Sis and have opened the door to a self-awareness and acceptance that I never thought possible, as well as inspired my actions of helping others become equally aware of who they are and the natural gifts, skills, and talents they possess. Past and present team members of Contagious Companies, particularly Janine, Frank, Bernice, and all of our coaches, remind me of the power of teamwork; and continue to give me the courage, conviction, and compassion to lead such a tremendous team of people, a gift I'm grateful for daily.

While it also goes without saying that there have been some difficult people that I, too, have wanted to make disappear (without going to jail, mind you), I'm grateful for the lessons they taught me that I've now been able to share with you. What would happen if we were all grateful for the lessons in life that seemed difficult at the time? Perhaps our perspectives would, in fact, be different. If you agree with that conclusion after reading this book, I thank you for seeing the larger vision I've tried to share. Thank you, dear reader, for embarking on a possible mind-set shift, for staying open to seeing others in a light you might not have considered before, and for sharing *Make Difficult People Disappear* with each and every person whom you believe it might make a difference for—and not only for them, but also for the world in which we live.

Introduction

Difficult people . . . no one goes through life without dealing with a few. Maybe they are loved ones, family members, colleagues, or even bosses. Whoever they are, dealing with them is complicated at best. Accepting them doesn't make the problem go away, but physically removing them from your life might have serious legal consequences. So, what's the solution? First, let's take a look at the origins of difficult people.

Certainly the concept originated long before any present-day people arrived on the planet. Hundreds of thousands of years ago, some people saw others doing things that weren't being done as they thought best, and they thought the others were *wrong*. Think of two cave dwellers arguing over how to build fire or make a wheel. Don't you think one of them got called wrong?

"Wrong" is a label, among many others, and it arises when someone is doing something that causes us stress. The person who sets something on your desk in the pile labeled *out-box* instead of *in-box*, is wrong. Same concept. Think about it. Some cave person likely wanted to set fire with their fancy new flame to whomever wanted to make the wheel square, just as we might daydream of bopping our annoying friend with our fancy new phone.

What you're probably wondering is not why people *are* difficult or how they *became* that way, but how to make them stop. You like your phone, and popular advice says bopping people is not good for the phone. Even if it might feel good for the soul at that moment, is it your best solution? Um, no. What should you do instead? Should you attend a class to learn to *deal* with difficult people, or maybe find a conference that teaches you how to *deal* with difficulty in general? Who wants to deal with it? It's a good start, but IF what you really want is to just make it go away and stop it from spreading to the team you lead, the family you love, and the friends or acquaintances you hang out with. Keep reading.

It would be tempting to offer a magic wand or pill or get-out-of-jail-free card with the purchase of the book you now hold in your hands, but alas it's just not that easy. Actually, it's easier.

Making all those difficult people disappear is really about attitude, awareness, and acceptance. It's the attitude that tells you to be fascinated instead of frustrated when someone cuts you off in traffic. It's the attitude that says "you can do this" when another project is added to your already monstrous to-do list. It's the awareness that pays attention to your own behavior, warning you when you start to act a bit difficult. It's the awareness that everyone in the world isn't walking around thinking about you and your behavior, but rather about their own and the issues in their day that are driving that behavior. It's the acceptance of the needs, preferences, tendencies, and natural-born traits of others who might be different than you, and it's the acceptance of the fact that people are not in fact difficult, but instead are . . .

Well, it wouldn't be right to give it all away before you've had a chance to read the story. If you want to make all those difficult people disappear, this is your ideal resource.

I've worked with countless leaders, teams, and organizations and have seen the results of changing your mind-set and it's effect on the presence of troublesome behavior. Leaders have used these strategies to help their teams work through having that one bad apple become the focus at the expense of taking care of a customer. They've used these principles to drop attrition rates by as much as 70 percent and radically reduce hiring costs by the millions. Frustrated employees have learned to work with others as a team instead of against each other as if in competition to see who can vent or sabotage the most.

What you will read in *Make Difficult People Disappear* will likely mirror situations in your own office. This fable looks at two days in the life of a manager who works with others, has a boss and a team, occasionally gets in her own way, and sometimes spends more time on difficult situations among those people than doing her work. She also has a life outside work, and while the fable takes place primarily in a business setting, you'll see that the wisdom provided is applicable to every part of your life, as well.

This book is a snapshot that will help you gather the details, follow a plan of action, and make swift changes that might be as simple as just stopping, starting, or continuing something consciously that you didn't realize you did in the first place. It will help you do things that will positively rub off on others and, seemingly simply and maybe magically, make their difficult behavior, and yours, disappear.

You see, what happens is that we all hear conversations differently; we also see situations and people's behavior differently. We are all looking through our own lens, and the picture we create of someone else is then captured and stored. We label that picture, and—because we live in a time of fast-moving information and programs and devices that ding, ring, and beep to get our attention and connect us to our lives—we simplify that label for easy reference and recall. It's not just the times we're in now. It seems to be how we've learned to "roll" automatically and it's time to do things differently. When we're focused on everything and everyone being so difficult, just as magically as we want the diffculty to disappear, more of it seems to show up.

Use this book as your easy reference to recall what to do next time you encounter a difficult person. Spread the word about how it works. Share the information with your family, church, team, organization, association, or simply your circle of friends. There's enough difficulty in the world to deal with right now. Why add dealing with difficult people to that effort? If we work together, maybe we can make all the difficult people, and even the silly, stupid, funny, or fascinatingly frustrating things they do, vanish into thin air as if by magic and without having to go to jail to make them disappear!

Author's Note on Sources

The CORE Multidimensional Awareness Profile® and the CORE Snapshot™ are registered trademarks of NaviCore International. It is with permission that references to this tool and its descriptions have been shared here. The CORE® Profile Online Evaluation book mentioned in Chapter 6 is made available to all who complete the CORE® Profile and purchase facilitation or coaching sessions. Monica Wofford, CSP, is a Certified CORE® Profile Facilitator and Coach and utilizes CORE® Profiles with coaching clients and as a measurement tool for the impact, behavior change, and ROI of training events.

Chapter 1

BRIBES . . . in the Form of Sprinkles?

Her hand floundered around the night-stand like a fish fresh out of water in search of the source for that horribly repetitive blaring sound. Finally, a forceful smack silenced the offending alarm clock. The noise stopped and abrupt silence followed. "There is a God!" she thought as she gathered her bearings. This morning was just like all the others and, after 15 years, she knew the drill: She'd hear the alarm. She'd get up. She'd feed the dog, make the coffee, wake their son, turn on the news, and then rush to take her own shower a full half hour before Dave would realize the world had woken up. Sometimes she was jealous of his ability to sleep through what could have been an Amtrak train barreling through their bedroom, but she also knew she didn't like the guilt that came with a late start in the morning. Anything after 6 AM was late for Cybil, even on the weekends.

But she also learned long ago that making him get up at the same time as her created a very "difficult" Dave. So she let it go, among a long list of other things that she ceased to worry about for her own sanity. It was her way of dealing with that difficulty, and she found that if she didn't ask much of him, the difficulty seemed to disappear, at least any that was expressed verbally. What went on in her head continued to be another story, but it just never seemed to bother Dave. She was the complete opposite of him, but he took it all in stride and loved her despite the times she treated other people in a way that he just couldn't imagine behaving.

As they did every morning, the voices in her head loudly told her to "look good under pressure" and "never let 'em see you sweat!" They swirled around as she thought of her to-do list and the international client e-mails that would have arrived during the night. Today was also the day she had to introduce the trainer for their full-day training class, "How to Make Difficult People Disappear." She truly believed the trainer was good, capable, and a good fit. She was funny, talented, and skilled, but Cybil still balked when she'd encouraged her to attend the class all day.

The irony was that she sometimes felt her mantra was, "I see difficult people," instead of "I see dead people" (from the movie *The Sixth Sense*), and she was pretty sure today would be no exception. Maybe it was because she'd shared her struggles with difficult people with this trainer, or for some other reason that the trainer convinced Cybil she needed to be in the class as an example to her team. She made it a point to emphasize how much value her attendance would have on the leadership in the organization, not to mention how much she would enjoy finding out how to make all those difficult people disappear.

"Why can't I just introduce you, leave, and come back at lunch?" she'd nearly pleaded in the early meetings, while trying to sound merely curious.

"It will work much better if you're there, Cybil. Otherwise, they'll get the impression this is nothing more than the campaign of the week. They won't do anything differently afterward. Besides, you and I both know that without rewards to entice them or consequences to deter them, people will do whatever is easiest for them. Do you remember that diagram I drew for you?" (See Figure 1.1.)

That was true. The leadership team always starts out with good intentions, but then, to reinforce the behavior, they have to provide continued feedback when people are getting off track.

The trainer continued, "Your being there and reinforcing the principles with your behavior will set up a reward-and-consequence system, of sorts. They'll get positive feedback from you if they do what they learn in class and negative feedback if you see them not doing what was taught in class. If you don't attend, you'll send the subtle message that it really doesn't apply to you or that you don't support it. Isn't there already enough us-versus-them behavior going on around here?"

"Okay, that makes sense. I'll be there," Cybil said, knowing the trainer was right, but it wouldn't be easy. She felt like the *us* in that "us-against-them" phrase was really "them against her" on some days.

Oh, the things she did for these people! The sacrifices she made for this team in trying to change, mold, modify, and grow! Why didn't they all just get it? Like now! Why did the people she led seem to need so much hand-holding from her? *"Just do your job! Get it done and stop the whining!"* she thought. Then again, she also knew most of them worked hard. A lot had changed in the industry, and some team members resented it and were acting out.

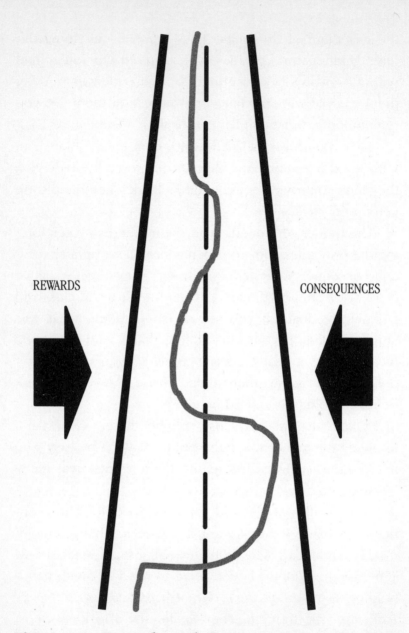

REWARDS

CONSEQUENCES

Figure 1.1 Rewards and Consequences to Motivate Performance

Make Difficult People Disappear

Some of them had become difficult, and she had shared as much with the trainer in their first meeting. She mentioned that she had a team member who was consistently negative and that no matter her best efforts to bond, be chatty, or build a rapport with this person, he seemed to walk around with a black cloud hanging over him.

She was running out of ideas for how to handle his sullen behavior. When during their first conversation the trainer gave her immediately applicable advice to combat the problem, Cybil decided to bring her in to train the entire team. The trainer told her to stop habitually saying "Hello, how are you?" to certain stressed-out people whom she knew would always answer negatively. Instead, the trainer suggested that she "just say hello and walk away." This little piece of advice made Cybil laugh out loud. How could something so simple make any difference? But she began to try this approach, and somehow, instead of her morning being filled with the 10 minutes of negative feedback she braced for daily, that difficulty disappeared.

The upcoming class was going to address this issue and others, while combining both a serious note and a sense of humor. As the trainer had told her, adults learn better when they're laughing. Based on how easy it had been for Cybil to put into practice a simple step that made her laugh loudly, she was convinced that was true. This class was the right thing to do, even if she still thought she'd regret a day of precious time away from her other work.

By the time Cybil finished her shower, where her brain continued to work overtime with no regard for her lack of a pen and paper, she'd only added four things to her to-do list. She used a notepad she kept in the bathroom for just such occasions (and secretly wished somebody would invent an underwater writing pad). As she wrote the last item, she heard Dave rustling to life. *Finally*, she thought. Ben arrived then, standing in the doorway, one eye open with arms stretched wide somewhere between a yawn and a contorted yoga pose.

"Hey, Mom?"

"Yeeeessss?" Cybil was always a little fearful of what the question would be at this hour in this morning.

"Did you bake the cookies last night?"

Her hand gripped the pen a bit more tightly. *"Cookies? What cookies?"* she thought. *"Did I bake cookies? What did I do last night? Wait, what's today? Did he tell me he needed me to bake cookies? Today?!"*

Her mind raced around looking for an answer that would work, but all of them sounded pathetic.

"I'm sorry . . . beg your pardon?" she replied, hoping maybe she misunderstood and he was talking about a girl named Cookie. Heaven forbid. Ben was only eight years old. But since she didn't remember baking any cookies, it was worth a try to find another possibility before she flipped out.

"The cookies for the bake sale today. The one that's gonna help us raise money for the animal shelter?" he sighed and mimicked the expression of the big-eyed Puss in Boots cat from the movies.

"You forgot, didn't you?"

"Can't I just give you money, Ben? I'm sorry, buddy, I don't remember you asking me to bake cookies, but I am

8

more than happy to make a donation directly to the animal shelter. Did you *tell* me you needed me to bake cookies?" Cybil was trying to sound like a concerned mom, but she realized she sounded more like a businesswoman trying to delegate.

Ben was such a charmer and so full of love, emotion, enthusiasm, and energy, but his attention span was the size of a tattoo on a gnat's behind. She knew it was highly likely and frankly probable that he forgot to tell her and that, somewhere between leaving the school building and getting into the car yesterday, he had completely forgotten about the cookies. It would not have been a surprise, and this wouldn't be the first time it had happened. Still, in her mind, good moms baked cookies. So this morning, she'd have to manage a workable solution and then later deal with the guilt of being a mom who worked long hours and missed these kinds of things.

"Yes, Mom, remember? I texted you yesterday."

He was right. It wasn't generous notice for cookie baking, but it was notice. She had completely forgotten the message that came in between a conference call, an interview, and an instant message from her boss. Cybil, master multi-tasker, had forgotten the message from her cute son who just needed some cookies. Surely June Cleaver wouldn't have missed that message. Heck, she didn't even work outside the house *or* have a phone *or* a boss! But what kind of mother puts an interview before her son? Oh boy. That was a conversation for her to have in her head another day. The reality was that she was a good parent, just really busy and sometimes unable to get it all done, including all

9

she expected of herself. It really bothered her when things like this happened. And it stressed her out for the rest of the day. Who knew guilt had so much power?

"Moooooooooom?" he asked, breaking the still silence, as she was contemplating a solution.

"Ben, I didn't bake the cookies and I completely forgot your message yesterday. I'm sorry, bud, but I'll take you to school this morning and we'll stop by our favorite bakery and pick up some cookies for the bake sale and maybe even a treat for you. Does that sound like a plan?"

She hated to use a bribe, but sometimes a treat smoothed the disappointment. Unfortunately, though, no treat was going to soothe the fact that the bakery trip would make her late for her 8 AM meeting at the office.

"Oh, wow! Okay. Can I get the ones with the special sprinkles on top? That'll be so cool! My cookies will be so much cooler than everyone else's! Awesome!" and off he went. Crisis averted. She had gone from "cookie monster" to "cool cookie mom" in a matter of moments. The next fire drill would be the call to her boss about the meeting and whatever excuse she could make up for being late. She wondered whether this one would be that easy and whether her boss might respond the same way if she mentioned "sprinkles." The positioning or maneuvering of things seemed to be one of her specialties.

To save time, her normally "big hair" went into an elegant clip, and within minutes of the cookie news she walked down the hall in search of Ben's choice for today's wild outfit. Bake sale or not, he was not allowed to wear some of his outfit choices in public. Hopefully, he had

10

chosen something that would bore her instead of bowl her over with laughter.

After outfit inspection, a quick meal of peanut butter and toast, and a kiss on the cheek to her freshly showered husband (who always seemed to be perplexed at the whirlwind Cybil created), they hopped in the car and headed to the bakery. As they pulled out of the driveway, she thought it would have been nice if Dave had made them breakfast instead of sleeping late.

As he watched them drive away, Dave thought it would have been nice if he'd let her wake up in peace instead of faced with the tornado in her brain that she seemed to consistently create and feel compelled to share.

She called her boss and gave a creative, but not completely untrue, reason for her tardiness. She said she needed to handle a family issue that, if not handled appropriately, would create a problem for the rest of her week. In her usual fashion, she turned an emotional issue into one that made logical sense. Her boss agreed that it was the right thing for her to do. He was a husband and a father, and though he was not by any means a fluffy, warm, touchy-feely man, Cybil knew how to approach him with logic and reason. It usually worked, and she could only hope the rest of the day would allow her to focus and get a few things done.

She was focusing on her office tasks, when bright shiny lights appeared behind her.

"You have got to be kidding me," she whispered as she made her way to the left shoulder within a block of the bakery. License and registration in hand, she hit the window button and nearly hung it out the window for the officer.

"Ma'am. Do you know why I pulled you over?"

"Honestly, I have no idea, but I'm sure you had a great reason. I'm on the way to Beth's Bakery and my son needs cookies and I have an 8 AM meeting and I'm running a little late this morning. Lots to do, but I'll try to be more careful, Officer. I am in a rush, so if you don't mind us working through this quickly, I'd appreciate it."

Sometimes she stunned even herself with her no-fear, get-it-done approach. Did she really just essentially tell an officer to make it snappy? Good grief.

"Well ma'am. If you'll give me a few minutes I'll see what I can do. Certainly, you're 'hurry' constitutes a need for driving 50 in a 35-mile-per-hour zone, and those cookies are one high priority. But I'm not sure they would hold up as a defense if you had an accident and hurt someone." There was just the slightest hint of sarcasm in his voice, and he talked at the speed of cold molasses being poured out of a jar. Ben's eyes were wide, and he was fascinated by the interaction.

"Well, hi there, young man. Are you the source of this urgent need for cookies?"

She thought, *Really? Do I look like a woman who has time to socialize? Just write me the ticket or let me go, and let's get this show on the road."* Fortunately, she knew when to keep her mouth shut . . . most of the time.

"We're going to get cookies with sprinkles and sell them at the bake sale to raise money for the animal shelter next to school! Do you have any animals at home? We used to have a cat, but she died. She was 23 years old!"

"Wow, that was some cat. I have a dog, but he doesn't eat cookies with sprinkles." They laughed, and by this time, Cybil's fingers began to tap the steering wheel as she contemplated walking to the bakery with Ben while Grandpa took his time in assessing her fine or processing her alleged offense.

The officer walked back to his car and, after what seemed like a mild eternity, returned with a warning. His reasoning was that he wasn't going to be the one who stood in the way of sprinkles that helped animals. Clearly, Ben had won his heart, as he did with everyone he met. Cybil admired her son's people skills and was grateful for one less thing to do later. She thanked the officer and tried not to speed off the shoulder like Mario Andretti on the way to the bakery.

The line at the bakery stretched out the door and seemed only to serve as a further test to Cybil's delicate patience. They stood in line and stood in line and stood in line after finding the only remaining parking space, which seemed a mile from the door. What was the deal this morning? Was everyone against her getting to the office and being productive? Clearly, she was still seeing difficult people. She was tempted to bribe the two women in front of them, but she didn't carry cash and didn't think sprinkles would work for them. Clearly, her rational and objective skills were waning.

Cybil tried not to rush Ben's decision when they reached the counter, and she counted to 10 a dozen times as the clerk made three mistakes and had to find a manager to help her with a bar code.

BRIBES . . . in the Form of Sprinkles?

"I'm so sorry, ma'am. These are a new item and I'm fairly new myself."

"Of course you are," she muttered, perhaps less than silently.

Had she been able to slow the car down and let Ben jump out, she would have. She loved her son, yet this morning was getting to be a bit ridiculous, and she wasn't laughing. She always felt that she could let far more slide at home than she could at work. At work, she'd have had no tolerance for this kind of thing and would have long ago lost it. She had that reputation, and she'd never been able to figure out why she couldn't just relax about things, or at least suppress them better at work, as she could at home. It was more than the fact that she loved her son and husband. She seemed literally to be two different people. One at home and one at work, and she wasn't sure which one took more energy to maintain, but she did know she was drained at the end of days like this. And many of her days were like this for one reason or another.

She pulled up to the school, kissed Ben, wished him luck on his bake sale, and tried not to rush his good-bye. He started to tell her a story about some project they were starting today, but she had to gently ask him to tell her later. The door closed and she was off. It was now 8:15, and traffic would make her office arrival before 8:45 a near impossibility.

She arrived at the office already exhausted and exasperated, but still outwardly composed, and saw her boss in the hall next to her office. His first gesture was to look at his watch and then at her. It was 8:45 and the class was to begin at 9:00.

"I'd prefer we try to meet at lunch if that works for you." He said with a bit of authority.

"I think that would be more effective, and I apologize, John. I had a few challenges this morning."

"Seems that way. We need to work on this project, but it can wait until lunch. By the way, the trainer is here and some of our folks are in the room already. Are you introducing her or am I?"

"I'll take care of it. In fact, I think she sent me her introduction. Let me get that, and I'll see you at lunchtime. I think we break at noon, and the food is already handled. Becca can coordinate all of that."

John nodded and strode down the hall, wondering when Cybil was going to stop "dealing with him" and just be herself. He wasn't sure what she always seemed to be guarding against, but he did know that it was hindering her ability to build rapport and trust on her team. She had such potential, if she could just let down the shield and sword and be a bit more approachable.

Cybil found the introduction, printed it out just before the low-toner light came on and did her best to nonchalantly stroll into the class, realizing that her intake of morning coffee and water were telling her she needed a detour. There was a full room of her teammates and participants from other departments, and she found the trainer at the front of the room. She shook the trainer's hand, appreciating the warm smile that seemed to acknowledge Cybil's frazzled start to the day, and took her cue when the trainer said, "I'm ready when you are."

The introduction was short and to the point, with a bit of humor that Cybil tried to deliver well, but thought she could have done better. *"Oh well,"* she thought, *"at least that part's done."* She settled into a chair in the back of the room and began to check her BlackBerry as the trainer began.

What she said caught her by surprise, as did the laughter from the rest of the room. It was something about being contagious and how attitudes are contagious and then a phrase that really caught Cybil's attention.

"Today, we'll look at those whom you work with and determine who's difficult and who's just different. We'll work on communicating with each person in a way they understand and in a way that, frankly, allows you to lead folks in a way that will encourage team members to stay longer, produce more, and complain less. The first place we want to start, though, is with your own ability to lead yourself. In my humble opinion, you must be able to first be yourself, and then lead yourself well, before you really have any business leading other people. So, let's start with *you.* Would you believe that most of our own leadership starts with the voices in our heads? In fact, who in here talks to themselves?"

Almost every hand in the room went up, and Cybil's BlackBerry found a spot on the table. She was intrigued and, at a minimum, thought this was going to be interesting. At least that is what the voices in her head said.

Of course, at this point, the voices were also saying, "Is it just me, or is everyone out there difficult?" She briefly

Make Difficult People Disappear

thought through the events of her morning. Between her husband, her son, the clerk at the bakery, the cop, her boss, and an incoming e-mail from China she had briefly seen, she was surprised she had actually managed to get something as simple as a cup of coffee without causing a problem that again slowed her down or presented itself as difficult. Was it a worldwide problem that everyone was either being purposely difficult, moving slowly, showing their stupidity or lack of thought, or was it just her? She began to feel her irritation rising and thought to herself, *"This lady had really better be good!"*

The trainer laughed along with the class when they saw how many talked to themselves. She even joked that we *all* talk to ourselves and that the more important question is usually, "How many voices are talking?"

At least she was funny, Cybil thought.

The trainer continued by asking the group another question.

"In fact, who in here has a voice inside your head that has convinced you that someone you work with is difficult beyond repair?" Very few hands went up, as people looked around the room and appeared to not wish to be known for talking about their colleagues.

"Well," said the trainer, "let me make this easier. Who in here has ever worked with someone, here or at another job, who literally reminded you of Eeyore from *Winnie-the-Pooh*?" This garnered laughter, and she continued.

"You know the type. You say 'Good morning' to this person and, much like the grumpy donkey in *Winnie-the-Pooh*, their only response is, 'What's good about it?'" She used a tone of voice that reminded Cybil so much of the difficult person she and the trainer had talked about, it was almost scary.

"There are going to be people you work with, live with, hang out with, or love who act like this. They will complain about their ice cream being too cold, about rain on a sunny day, or about having to work too hard to get exactly what they want in life—and that's okay. I want you to immediately think of who these folks are and then imagine, next time you see them, that they've just come into the office, gone to their proverbial locker, taken out their Eeyore suit, unzipped it, stepped into it, and are now walking around with two ears and a tail all day long!" The room burst into laughter at the visual, and she definitely had their attention.

So far, the trainer hadn't made any difficult people disappear, but in the first 15 minutes she had connected with the class and engaged the room. It was working, and it made Cybil believe that whatever this woman would say just might not land on deaf ears, unlike what she herself had tried to do for months.

It also sounded like there were going to be some applicable tools that all of them could use to make difficult people, or at least their perception of them as difficult, disappear, without having to go to jail and without Cybil having to bribe them all with sprinkles.

For videos and more information that will enhance what you've learned in this chapter, go to: www.MakeDifficult PeopleDisappear.com.

Chapter 2

SHIFTS . . . in Your Expectations

Cybil settled into the class comfortably, willing to reconsider her initial perception that it would be a waste of her day. She had already learned a lot from this instructor in the short time she'd known her.

The instructor continued with her Eeyore example and made it relevant to the group by encouraging them to use the visual, and also by explaining that making difficult people disappear started *within yourself* instead of with *other people*. The instructor then went over the day's learning objectives. First, they were going to understand themselves a bit better. Then they would learn how they could sometimes be perceived as difficult, and if *they* were that way, then this might also be the reason for others' suffering from the same perception. Then they would work on applying specific methods to put this knowledge into practice and overlap with what they already knew about relationships and communication with others. One by one, Cybil secretly confirmed that each objective on its own would have made her day if they'd put it to use. Each would help her deal with the difficulties in her own world, even though she already thought she had a pretty good handle on understanding herself and the needs of those she worked with.

She was distracted for a moment by her BlackBerry as it vibrated for about the fifteenth time and kept shaking the entire table. She pushed the button to put it on silent mode. Soon after, her temptation to check it actually waned and then almost disappeared, at least for a few moments.

Then it hit her. She wondered how the bake sale was going. She wondered whether Ben was feeling supremely cool with his sprinkled cookies. Then she wondered what Dave was doing by this time. He was normally very laid back and didn't get going until later in the morning, and his job afforded him that luxury. Dave was a graphic artist who created amazing artwork, particularly if left alone during the time he needed to create it.

Cybil had never understood why someone of Dave's talent had no initiative to go after bigger accounts, focus on building his own business, or create something larger than his comfortable drafting table in his home office. For the first few years of their marriage, she had tried to push and had offered to help and work with him. It just wasn't his style, and she respected the demeanor he took with her the night he gently told her this was his career decision. She had her career in the style that worked for her, and this was how he liked to work. Besides, if both of them of were working 300 hours a week, who would take care of Ben? She understood and threw all of her efforts into her son and into her work. She let go of the need for her husband to be ambitious, but she secretly missed what she thought would be an opportunity to have a high-powered partner at home whom she viewed as an equal in that area and who immediately garnered her respect. There were worse things, and he was a great father and good to her emotionally, though she didn't need that nearly as often as he thought. Her greatest struggle was respecting what he did—or rather, how he went about his work life—when she was in her full-force, get-things-done mode.

To his credit, Dave was the only man who had seen through her self-imposed barriers and who wanted to spend time with her despite her tirades and frustration with the seeming difficulty of the world and the people in it. Dave seemed to love her for who she was and even joked that he loved watching "the show" when she became heated and wanted to rant at someone. He wasn't sure if it was a show or a tornado, but as long as it wasn't directed at him, he was fine.

Cybil realized she was daydreaming as the class erupted in laughter. The trainer had just asked if anyone in the room *wanted* to work with difficult people, which she put in air quotes with her fingers. She then asked if any of those difficult people, or "Eeyores," as she had called them, were in the room. What she said next made everyone laugh.

"If they're in here, then all eyeballs up front. Look at me. There's no need to point them out or stare!" She did have a humorous and engaging way of training and capturing everyone's attention. It wasn't due to the trainer that Cybil's mind wandered; it was something she had done all her life and that had gotten her in trouble often. It was one of the reasons she worked so hard at staying focused, particularly when there were numbers involved. Thankfully, she was gifted in multitasking and in catching up quickly if she did miss something. Or did she miss things once she felt she got the point and then thrive off the pressure of catching up?

"A wandering mind does not calculate accurately," her accounting professor had told her, looking sternly look over the tops of his glasses, as he informed her of the C on her final exam. She couldn't seem to help it even now, but tried very hard to keep it hidden and to a minimum, more so because of her fear of what others thought than because of what she thought she would actually miss.

But to answer the trainer's question, no, of course she didn't choose to work with difficult people. She just thought they were part of the reality of her job and her life. She had worked with a few and remembered feeling as though she had married one for the first few years of her marriage, until she let go, which is exactly what the trainer recommended next.

"Most people aren't difficult by nature. They're different, and we make them difficult by expecting them to be just like us and then choosing to see them as difficult when they aren't. We then label them as difficult, and it becomes the explanation we use for their behavior, so that everything they do, we see through the filter of that explanation. It's part of our culture to see the behaviors of others who might not look like or act like us as wrong, and it's more prevalent for some personalities than others, but it all begins with what we expect them to act like, look like, and be like. The reality is that if common sense were common, everyone would have some and wouldn't you agree that what is common sense for some might not make sense for others?" Most in the room nodded in contemplative and then collective agreement. "Now, on a different note, I ask you, if you looked up a Jack Russell breed of dog in the dictionary expecting to find a picture and the description of a regal, assertive, strong-willed German shepherd, would you be disappointed?"

Several heads didn't nod or move side to side, but rather cocked sideways like confused puppies. Cybil just wanted to know the point, but she thought she may have gotten it already.

The trainer continued, "If you really expect to see a German shepherd and read about a German shepherd when you look up a Jack Russell, chances are you'll be disappointed, but not because the dog (or the dictionary, in this case) is wrong, but because we expected something that wasn't realistic and chose to continue those expectations even after clarifying the difference between, in this case, the two breeds of dog. How often do you look at your 'difficult' coworkers and expect them to do the same things you would do, when you know that is not their style or standard behavior? Are you labeling them as difficult because of their fault or your own disappointment? Are you choosing to insist that they do what you would do, even when you know better, and then punishing them for their actions anyway?"

She went on to share that most had adopted the age-old Golden Rule as their guiding principle for communication and interaction with others. The Golden Rule, by most interpretations, states, "Do unto others as you would have them do unto you," and while in theory that seems like a nice way to behave, the trainer suggested it didn't work in communication.

By insisting that others communicate only in the way we want to receive communication, simple pleasantries

25

aside, we miss the fact that they may need or prefer a different type or style of communication and delivery. They might have different expectations. They might prefer e-mail, whereas you prefer phone or face-to-face communication. They might prefer direct and to the point, whereas you prefer to talk socially for a moment or being more subtle about getting down to business.

Her suggestion was to instead adopt what she referred to as the Platinum Rule, developed by a man named Tony Alessandra. The Platinum Rule states, "Do unto others as they would want to be done unto." It made sense and also made Cybil laugh when she conjured up the visual of a German shepherd treating a Jack Russell as if it were a fellow German shepherd. Combining the earlier metaphor and this concept of the Golden and Platinum Rules, she could see the smaller dog jumping up and down saying, "Hey, I'm down here! Hey!" It made her laugh, but also seemed to make a valid point. How many of her peers had she blindly treated as *she* wanted to be treated without consciously considering what it was *they* needed, or how they needed her message to be delivered?

■ ■ ■

Cybil wondered for a moment what her mom saw when she looked up her oldest daughter's name in the diction-ary. It was a strange place for her mind to go right now, but the instructor was correct in her assumptions, she *did* talk to herself. It was something she didn't talk about often, but Cybil and her mom did not speak often, either. In fact, they had not had a solid relationship since her childhood, and much of what she remembered since that time was her mother calling her unflattering names or being critical of what she did. She told Cybil she was too strong, too aggressive, too direct, too bossy, too domineering, too controlling, or too argumentative; her mother then criticized her strength, telling her to tone it down at every opportunity. She even told her that she was too driven, that she should relax. Cybil was always *too something*, and consequently being told to relax had become a trigger for anxiety and reactive behaviors

In fact, nothing she did after going from the natural dependencies of a small child to some independence as an adolescent seemed right for either of her parents. Their extreme criticisms made her start to believe all the negative things they said about her, and unfortunately she began to act that way. She didn't really think it was who she was, but she'd heard the drumbeat so many times that she had created a familiar rhythm of behavior.

When she and Dave discussed these things, it seemed that Dave had a similar, but opposite, experience. His parents, or at least his dad, had always told him to "suck it up," and he tried to be that way for a while, but it just never felt right. Instead of spending years fighting what he thought was right, he just let go. He let go of the need to please his father; he let go of the need to act stronger and be that man who was more filled with bravado and take-charge behavior than he felt was necessary. He quickly, far more quickly than Cybil, learned to be comfortable in his own skin.

It was actually a wonder Cybil had gotten to where she was with such heavy programming on not being

27

good enough (or, as it translated in her childhood brain, *unlovable*). The lack of comfort in her own skin was what she suspected was the driving force behind many of her lashing-out reactive behaviors. It seemed to be the old fight-or-flight principle, and her personality wouldn't let her run away from a struggle, so she fought, even when there wasn't one. It was as if her parents wanted a nice, quiet, fluffy bunny and what they saw in her instead was a pit bull.

To make matters worse, Cybil was still desperately trying to be that softer and fluffier version of herself. She wanted to be someone who would walk away or flee from someone's criticism instead of standing to fight, thus validating their accusation of her behavior or personhood. Some of it stemmed from her upbringing, she was sure. Didn't everyone have at least some issues with their upbringing? She paused for a moment to address the question in her mind.

"Well, almost everyone did," she thought, *"except that girl in high school she knew who . . .* focus, *Cybil!"* Gosh, those voices in her head and distractions were annoying!

What didn't stem from her upbringing was the experience she came back to each time personality profiles were involved, and she planned to talk with the trainer about it when it came time to facilitate her in-depth results later that afternoon. Cybil dreaded it, actually. . . . In her mind it was 90 minutes to talk all about how broken she was and what was wrong with her (again).

She remembered, as if it were yesterday, the first time she did a personality profile. The company she worked

Make Difficult People Disappear

with in her early 20s had set up an opportunity for all the managers to complete the Myers-Briggs profile. It really wasn't an "opportunity," as the exercise was mandatory and also included peer feedback. It felt like an oncoming execution without live ammo, but she had to do what she had to do to get ahead.

When her time came to receive the feedback and call the facilitator, she couldn't find a quiet space in her office, which at that time consisted of a cubicle, so she hopped in her car to combine lunch with learning. Had she known to call it a "lunch and learn" back then, she would have. For all she knew, she invented the concept trainers talked about regularly now, but likely not. She also didn't know that her "lunch and learn" was about to turn into a "learn and burn."

When in her car, the facilitator asked her to pull over, which she thought was odd, but she said she wanted Cybil to read the documents along with her. It seemed an excessively detailed exercise in which she was being painted into a corner of being "too strong" and "too bossy," and now this facilitator was going to exercise some control. She went through each painstaking detail as Cybil sat in the parking lot of a building down the street from her office—and then the words she would remember forever were spoken.

The facilitator said, "There's a lot of good feedback here, and I would strongly encourage you to take heed and pay attention to some of it, because if you keep going down this path, no one's going to want to work with you. It's almost as if your calm-side switch is broken and you slip into anger and a reactionary mode very quickly.

29

It really doesn't work well and is something I would recommend you fix."

She'd heard this all her life, and it crushed her every time. It was the repeated message that who she was wasn't good enough or worth loving and had to be fixed. She *wanted* to be softer. She *wanted* to be kind and gentle and loving and have a reputation for never saying a cross word, but the more she tried to be sweet, the more she ran into stupid ideas or slow people or things that clearly didn't make sense to her but that others seemed to buy into with ease.

She felt obligated to help people understand what they were looking at and how to avoid making a mistake, how to do better next time, and how to grow from the experience. Wasn't that what bosses did? Wasn't that what good friends did? Wasn't that even what good Samaritans did? For example, she remembered vaguely explaining to a convenience store clerk that he could be so much more efficient if he'd stop chatting it up on the phone when he had a line that extended out the door. She saw her remarks as a service to those in line, yet they saw her only as a rude woman who had lost her mind.

Yet here was a professional telling her she was broken. It was official now. Her parents weren't just mean or crazy or speaking from their own issues. It was Cybil. She didn't say much to the facilitator, who thankfully couldn't see the fear, tears, and sadness in her face. In fact, after those comments, she recalled saying something like, "I'll work on it. Thanks for your time," after which she disconnected the call and sobbed for the rest of her lunch hour.

Though the experience had happened 20 years ago, it was a day she would remember for years to come. There was no room for the facilitator to be wrong. It was clear confirmation of the message she had heard for decades and was based on the most popular tool at the time and delivered by a professional, even if that tool and the facilitator seemed to synthesize the information about someone without ever addressing what to do with that information. The trainer had assured her this would not be the case with the tool they were using now.

However, since that expereince, she had tried diligently, with every coach, class, book, and barker of self-help services, to fix herself and become a better, more lovable person. In fact, it had been an initial barrier that held her back from bringing in this new trainer. The trainer had somehow sensed that there was a bravado and guardedness about Cybil that, once people saw through it, could be easily overlooked. In fact, the trainer had overlooked it, and there had been an instant chemistry between them, but Cybil was not sure how she had seen through the armor when so many others had not or could not.

Cybil had mellowed somewhat over the years, and this new trainer came across as someone who would be a bit more objective, but she had also said something that stuck with Cybil and helped her make the decision.

Before hiring her, Cybil asked the trainer to present information on the process to the leadership team. Cybil couldn't help but still feel skeptical of trainers and personality assessments. "This profile," the trainer suggested as she pointed to a sample report in the final decision-making meeting, "is designed to show our developed areas and those that elude us. It is not a tool that only identifies strengths and *weaknesses*," she said with a sarcastic voice and demonstrative eye roll, "but instead shows us how we react on an average day and what behaviors we use, and in what order, under increasing amounts of stress. I assume that you've managed to live your life just fine up until this point and managed to cope with any areas of underdevelopment without my input, so for me to tell you or anyone else that you have weaknesses that need to be changed would be silly."

After pausing to allow the team to process the information, she continued, "We'll look at the report and identify, what, if anything, isn't working for you. If you don't like something, we'll seek to modify that behavior and give you the techniques and skills to do so. If you like everything you see, then this will merely be informative and raise your awareness, and that will be true for everyone who completes the profile. It's quite a unique tool and process. Most people have immediate epiphanies, particularly if they have been faking who they are for some time and are getting tired of the energy it takes."

The leadership team reacted with caution and skepticism to the idea of the program, but reluctantly agreed. Cybil had chimed in by saying, "I completely understand, and tell me about it. Being who you are not is exhausting!" There were a few looks from the other leaders as she realized how much passion had come out in her comment, but she tried to regain composure and ignore them by asking a few more questions. "How long does it take to complete, and which managers are we granting access to this tool and the time to complete it?" These were the only questions she thought needed to be asked. Her mind was at ease with her passion and the way in which she just moved forward to the needed information. Perhaps for more personal reasons than she was willing to reveal, she felt this choice of training initiative would result in better leadership and more awareness of and on the team she led. Though she did still have a modicum of trepidation about her own profile facilitation and her sensitivity to criticism, for some reason, she trusted this woman.

Cybil was beginning to realize intellectually that just because someone else thought something about her, that didn't make it true or mean she had to believe it. Although knowing something intellectually and really feeling and believing it were apparently two different things, she still struggled with this more often than she was willing to admit.

■ ■ ■

There was a sudden chatter in the class that brought Cybil back to the room rather abruptly. She had no idea how long she had been "out to lunch," but Jason, the company CFO, who was seated next to her, was looking at her with an expectant expression of "Are you ready?" Apparently, they had been asked to find a partner, and Cybil had no idea what for or what to do with her new partner. Jason explained the exercise to her and she quickly caught on, thankful for her ability to assimilate information at a rapid rate. The information involved thinking of a personal or professional goal about which they were excited. They had been asked to think about it, visualize it, and even feel how they would feel when they accomplished it to the extent they were able.

Cybil was thinking about her goal, within the next five years, of having her boss's job, and just then the trainer shared the rest of the instructions that she'd held back while everyone envisioned their goals. She asked them to share the goals out loud with their partner and then asked, as if on cue from Cybil's until now nonexistent telepathy skills, whether anyone needed more time to come up with a new goal. The room erupted loudly with cackles and squeals of delight.

Cybil wasn't sure what everyone else's goals were, but at least she wasn't the only one uncomfortable with sharing hers out loud. She quickly came up with the goal of making sure Ben went to college and was a success in whatever he wanted to do. She fervently hoped he had more ambition than his father and was already seeing signs of that, but one just never knew what would happen after adolescence, and he was already a handful at age eight. As she continued this train of thought, Cybil became more excited and passionate about her hopes for her young son; then the trainer asked them all to share their new goals with a partner, and to do so as if they were angry.

It was an odd request, but, as she demonstrated, they were all to act as if they were mad about whatever their goal was or to express it to their partner using anger while talking about this passionate personal goal. There were some valiant efforts, but the room just kept erupting in giggles that escalated until the trainer finally interceded.

"Wait a minute. Wait a minute! I thought the assignment was to share your goal as if you were angry?" She paused to wait for the room to calm down.

"Then how come all I hear is a bunch of laughter?"

She continued to attempt to get the group back to silence, and then she asked a question in a very quiet voice. Everyone quieted down to hear her near whisper.

"Why is this so difficult?"

The answers varied: "We like this person," "Because I'm not mad," "Goals are supposed to be positive." Then the trainer went on to make the point.

"So, I'm curious. If it's this hard to act in negative manner about a goal that is deeply positive to you, don't you think the same thing works in the reverse?"

There was a calm, reflective silence in the room as they all thought about the connection between how their attitude reflected what was in their mind whether they liked it or not. It was nearly frightening to think about how good most of them had gotten at being falsely positive and smiley at the office, even when what was in their head was negative. The trainer pointed out that people could always tell . . . if they were paying attention. Of course, as she also pointed out, people weren't always paying attention.

The trainer then made her final point of the morning: If you are utterly convinced that someone is difficult, in most cases you are going to treat that person as if they are difficult—no matter what he or she does. She followed up by telling a personal story about how she had lost 35 pounds one year and went home for Christmas only to have her mom say she still looked heavy. Apparently, her mother had seen her that way all her life. It was her mother's deeply held belief that her daughter was heavy, despite the insurmountable evidence that she no longer fit that description. The trainer then asked a rhetorical question. "How many deeply held beliefs are you hanging on to that are keeping you from seeing anything other than difficult people?"

So far, all of Cybil's team members and the other participants in this session seemed pleased that they had taken a day out of their work to spend in a classroom. That was one hurdle she would not hear about later on, thankfully, and that would at least reduce the number of difficult people she would have to deal with on this topic. Then again, would she still choose to see them as difficult, no matter what they said to her? Could she get rid of her own well-ingrained expectation and beliefs?

The trainer called for a 16-minute break. Yet again, the room chuckled, this time at the odd time choice. She had said earlier that adults learn more when they're laughing, and somehow she was able to combine comedy with training. It wasn't just a motivational show. It was a learning experience in which the time flew by and powerful points slipped in without the normal resistance to change or new information that compelled one to take new actions. Cybil wasn't sure how an hour and half had already passed, but then again she had been daydreaming. Now, however, she needed to address e-mails and end-of-day reports from overseas.

Back at her desk and just as she clicked on the report from the UK office, her cell phone rang. Her sister's picture was on the screen, and part of Cybil thought she would just grab it later because now wasn't a good time. It was a conflict she wrestled with often when her sister called. She loved her younger sister and yet couldn't help considering her needy. She conceded and decided to answer.

"Hey there, Sis. I'm on a quick break from a training class, but what's up?"

Sometimes dropping the hint of a time constraint worked, but more often than not, it opened the door for unlimited talk time with equally limitless apologies for the time she took. Cybil never understood what part of "I'm in a hurry" wasn't clear, but then again, she chose to pick up the phone.

"Oh, okay. Well, it's okay. It's just been a rough day, and I thought maybe I could talk with you about it. I know you're busy. It's okay." Simone sounded as if her favorite dog had died, and Cybil knew the guilt tactic well after years of experience with her sister, but never had learned how to avoid getting sucked into it without feeling even more guilt.

Cybil really just wanted to say, "Well, can you get to the point of the problem so I can help you fix it or figure out that there isn't any way I can help?" Yet an admonition rolled around in her head telling her to do the obligatory listening thing. She wasn't coldhearted, but simply didn't quite know how to spell *empathy*, particularly with Simone's Chicken Little ("The sky is falling!") problems. Cybil could overcome bigger obstacles in her 16-minute lunch break than Simone had seemingly overcome in a year or more . . . but (and it was a big *but*) this was her sister.

Consistent in her effort to coach Simone in getting to the point, she urged, "Well, honey, tell me what's going on real quick. Maybe I can help." Simone answered, "It's Philip. I think he's having an affair."

The only word that came to mind to describe her sister's long-time boyfriend was the back end of a donkey, and it was the sum total of her reaction at this point as well, but she knew that wouldn't fly with Simone.

"What do you mean you *think* he's having an affair? Did you catch him in an awkward position?" Cybil, whose office door was wide open, was well aware that screaming, "That donkey's bottom!" (or other choice words) would not help her image at work, while also laughing in her own head about how her expressions had changed since she'd had Ben. There was a time not so long ago when she'd have let far worse words fly forth from her lips.

"He's working late and calling me less and seeming less interested in my day lately. I'm not sure what to do."

"Sis, listen to me. If he is having an affair, you and I will work through this and you'll come out on top, I promise. I want you to go out and enjoy something fun for yourself. Go get a pedicure or go to the mall and give yourself some retail therapy, sweetheart. Take your mind off of things. My suspicion is he's just busy at work and having a hard time conveying how he feels when he's overwhelmed. Remember how I get when I'm really focused on a project? In fact, like right now, I've got to get back to this class. I love you, honey, and I want to hear all about your feelings and more details and see what we can do. Can we do that later tonight? I'll call you on my

38

way home. I'm sure Philip is doing the same thing and just doesn't realize how much you'd like for him to just pick up flowers or show you some love. Isn't his love language different than yours? Didn't you read that book together and discover that you need words of affirmation and gifts and he needs physical affection, or something like that? His mind is just deeply involved in his work and too tired to be affectionate, and he's going back to what is natural for him without stopping to think about what you need. Isn't he building a new mall or metropolis or next universe of some sort?"

Philip was an important architect in Boston and seemed to always have his head in a project, but it allowed Simone to use her artistic talents and not be the starving artist that she would have been without Philip's financial success. Cybil was aware of the possibility that he might have strayed and yet hoped for her sister's sake, and his own hide, that he was just doing what she usually did when she was slammed with work. It made her grateful that Dave didn't ask for as much attention as Simone. It was odd how they were so similar and yet so different sometimes. She sometimes seemed needier than Cybil thought she should be, and certainly more needy than Cybil would let anyone see in herself, but then again it seemed to have worked for them for years. This wasn't the first time Simone had entertained this kind of suspicion; had it happened to Cybil, she'd have been on the next flight to her husband's business trip destination or driven to his lunch appointment and called him on the carpet immediately. She really did not have patience for lies, but she would also have likely overreacted and caused more damage than a high-powered and high-profile member of Boston society like Philip would have been willing to put up with.

It had been the story of Cybil's life. She had often been labeled difficult because she took charge, handled things, got the answers she needed, and stayed strong in the face of danger, perceived or otherwise. What most didn't know is that she fell apart in private and that there had been many times when she fell apart with the help of half a carton of Häagen-Dazs as her personal therapy tool. Whereas Simone went directly to the falling-apart stage, and no one believed she could get through a crisis on her own. Cybil, the big sister, was always her go-to person. Little had changed since their childhood, and sometimes Cybil grew tired of having to be the strong one all the time. Wasn't there anyone who understood who she was and what she needed, someone who had the strength for her to lean on once in a while?

"But what if he is? What will I do?"

"Honey, we don't know if he is or isn't, and I really can't get into it right now. Will you go do what I've suggested? Maybe go have lunch with some of your girlfriends from the museum?"

"They are all busy, but yeah, that's fine. I'll try to keep my mind off of things. I'm sorry I bothered you, sis. I know how busy you are."

"Simone. Stop it. You know I always care about what is going on with you and I'm always here for you. If you were on fire or bleeding or in trouble, you know I'd be on the next flight out. It's just that I really don't think this is what you think it is. Okay, hon? I've gotta run, but I'll call you on my way home from work."

Simone hung up hesitantly, and Cybil's mind wandered for a moment about what had happened this time to give Simone that impression. It was something she'd have to "rotate around to the back," so to speak, and compartmentalize until later. She had to get back to class, and it wasn't on her list today to kick her brother-in-law's butt, but she would make the time for it later if she needed to. He really was a good guy. Cybil simply didn't always have the time to pick up Simone's pieces when his style didn't meet her emotional needs.

As she walked back down the hall toward class, having accomplished none of what she wanted in her short break, it dawned on her that she had always chosen to see her sister as not someone who was difficult, but as someone who needed her. Cybil wasn't sure what she would do or how she would feel if her sister no longer showed a need to rely on her strength.

By the same token, why did she label employees on her team who acted just like her sister as "whiny," "pouty," "weak," and, of course, "difficult"? Had she chosen to see them that way and chosen to see Simone through a less than difficult filter? It was beginning to appear as if that was the case, but Cybil wasn't sure why. She was sure she wanted to find out. In fact, she expected to find out, but then she reined in her expectations. If she expected the trainer to do something she hadn't planned on, then Cybil would see the class as missing something. She would see the Jack Russell when she was looking up "German shepherd."

Cybil made a mental note to ask the trainer whether she planned to address how we choose to label the same behavior, but in different people, differently. She decided quickly that asking whether those elements would be included would be far more productive than assuming they would be and spending energy on disappointment. It was amazing to her how much she'd become aware of the power of her expectations.

For videos and more information that will enhance what you've learned in this chapter, go to: www.MakeDifficult PeopleDisappear.com.

Chapter 3

LABELS . . . That Actually Make Sense

Sixteen minutes later, class started up again. She could tell because the door closed and something told her this was not the time to exercise her authority and stay out of the class to handle one more e-mail. Plus, it assuaged some guilt to run back into class just as she had told her sister she would. Right on time, as the trainer began, Cybil quietly slipped in and took her seat. She met eyes with the trainer and returned her smile.

"So, let's take a closer look at all those difficult people you work with. No names and no pointing, unless you want to point at yourselves. Have you come to the realization that in some cases you might be . . . hmmm . . . let's see, how do I say this . . . part of the problem?" She said it with just enough playful sarcasm that we got the point, yet didn't feel as though she'd singled us out. Something about the added levity made palatable the suggestion that we caused our own difficult interactions with our choices, perceptions, and expectations.

"The reality is," she proceeded after waiting for buy-in from most of us, "that we aren't difficult, and neither are those folks in your head right now whom you *wanted* to point to earlier this morning. Sometimes just knowing that can make some of your difficult people disappear, but there's more to it than just knowing that information."

She continued, "It's important to realize that we are different from each other in some significant ways of behaving and communicating. It's more than just seeing physical differences. We think, and thus respond, react, and communicate, differently to the same situations. You'll begin to see that more when we each talk in detail about your own CORE Multidimensional Awareness Profile®, or what we call the CORE MAP. But before we each have a chance to talk individually, let's look at some of the differences between the trait sets of Commander, Organizer, Relater, and Entertainer, the descriptive preference labels that make up the acronym CORE in the CORE Snapshot™ that I placed on your tables while you were on break [see appendix]. This CORE Snapshot™ handout is merely an introduction and very abbreviated version of the comprehensive online CORE MAP. We use it for in-class and training purposes only, and it helps to lay the foundation for what you will learn in your 90-minute facilitation of your more detailed individual CORE MAP results. Please keep in mind, it doesn't reveal nearly as much detailed information or how-tos as the online tool we'll each talk about individually, but it can at least tell us your dominant behavior right now (or at least the one you think is most dominant). What it *won't* tell us in the 18 rows of word choices is who you likely are authentically, how you handle stress, and whether you have been faking who you are for so long that your behaviors have become conditioned and habitual. In other words, if you've been 'faking it until you make it' on a daily basis and no longer know it, we won't know that for sure until we're in our one-on-ones. Have you any of you ever faked anything?"

The trainer blushed as giggles began to fill the room. She quickly added, *"Behavior-wise*, that is"* but it was too late to recover from her unintended double entendre.

"Okay, okay. Wow! That likely isn't how I need to say that in the future, but you know what I mean. Let's lay the groundwork for your one-on-one session by having you complete this handout. If you will, please, choose one word per *row* that accurately describes your behavior, at least today. I repeat: one word per *row*."

She placed great emphasis on the word *row*, and everyone seemed to get it and didn't quite understand her repeated emphasis. Cybil then glanced at Jason's paper, since he'd already started answering while the trainer explained it, and almost burst out laughing. The trainer had given them all permission to gesture with arms stretched from left to right and to say the word *row* in slow motion if they saw someone with only four words on the page. This would indicate that they had confused a row with a column and needed a refresher on those terms. Cybil looked at Jason, tapped him on the shoulder, and said as slowly as she could, "Rrrrrooooooooooowwwww."

He looked at her quizzically. Cybil traced her finger across the top row and the four words in it and then pointed to the three words on the page that Jason had chosen thus far. It was as if a lightbulb had been turned on over his head. He shook his head, laughing at himself, and began at the top row of the page.

The trainer then shared with the class, "I hear we've just had our first *row* educational lesson. Great job . . . and thanks, Cybil. Not to worry, Jason. It happens all the time.

LABELS . . . That Actually Make Sense

Oh, and if you struggle with picking one word that best describes you in any given row, you are also welcome to choose the word that is the least offensive."

She gave them ample time to complete the Snapshot™ handout and then invited them to review the information in each quadrant on the other side of the page. It was amazing how many people were nodding their heads in agreement and laughing at the accuracy of the results of something so simple and short. Cybil thought just for a moment how nice it would be if they all laughed this easily at other times when these kinds of differences came up.

"All right, let's take a look at these together. You've seen your results and shared them with your neighbor, I suspect, but I want to add more depth and information to what you're starting to see. Remember, the titles of the four quadrants on your page are just descriptive labels for a behavioral trait set, and before we go any further, I must give you a few caveats. It is not our purpose in talking about these today to label you as a whale, a lion, a lamb, or a peacock—or red, green, yellow, or blue. There are a plethora of tools out there, that are derived from the four-quadrant behavioral model, developed by Hippocrates in 400 BC. Other assessments originate from Carl Jung's work with preferences. The challenge is that somewhere along the way, the well-intended verbiage used by most tools to help us understand preferences and behaviors has morphed into definitive labels, stating, for example, that we *are* a 'Lion' or a 'Director' or 'Red.' The truth is that you are all four personality preferences, to some degree, no matter their label, if you brought your whole brain with you today. You're likley

48

Make Difficult People Disappear

seeing this with the scores that show up in each column. You will also see this in more detail in the full reports later."

The room laughed out loud, and some even accused colleagues of never bringing their whole brain to the office. This idea also made Cybil think. She had been told she was one type. What if all these years, the person who told her that information had been wrong? Why had she never really considered that option until now?

After the laughter subsided, the trainer continued, "Considering everyone appears to have brought their whole brain and whole head with them, most of you will have scores higher than zero in all four columns or quadrants. Even if you have columns with no score, you will at least be able to see that there are times that you behave in ways that fit every column. There will be one that is more natural to you, or perhaps one that you have developed more than another, but there will not be any name tags, desk plates, or things hanging outside your door that say you are a particular something, after this class nor in the future. That's just silly labeling. You are a well-rounded being who can be any and all of these preference, or trait set labels. However, you will be dominant in one of the labels, secondarily dominant in another, third most dominant in another, and what is called *dormant* in another. One will be more natural to you than the others, and it is the one you do without thinking and that most of us demonstrate when we're stressed or angry. If you have a high degree of self-awareness already, this will likely be the one in which you have your highest column total. Make sense?"

Wow. Did it ever! This was new information that Cybil had never heard of or considered. Myers-Briggs was not the only profile she'd ever taken, and she was curious about why she hadn't heard this anywhere before. It made such complete sense and explained why she often couldn't figure out how to label some people. She was becoming much more curious to see the results of her own profile after class.

"So, let's talk about that first quadrant and add a bit more detail to the theories that I keep alluding to this morning. What is the label we use in the first quadrant?"

They all said "Commander" and then listened and laughed as she described the Commander set of behaviors as the one that was ambitious, focused, often overachieving, and often motivated by the phrase "get it done." "For Commanders, nearly everything and everyone in their world is considered either an inhibitor or a contributor to their productivity. It's how they operate, and it doesn't mean they are cold or insensitive, it means they are task-driven. If you want something done, give it to a Commander."

This sounded indicative of Cybil's high score and daily behavior. She had almost an entire column of words checked off in the Commander column. Then the trainer said something beyond poignant. It was something that nearly knocked Cybil out of her chair, as though the woman had read her mind, but it also made her rethink some of what she'd been told and to reconsider for a second time whether she'd always been telepathic, or just in this class. It was a little spooky how in sync she was with this trainer.

"Now, before we go any further, I must share a secret with the women in the room just for a moment. Gentlemen,

I apologize, but I hope you'll allow me some latitude. Ladies, the Commander label and behavior is *not*, and I repeat, *not* synonymous with the big B word. If you have a high score in this column, it does not mean you ride your broom into the office every day or that you need a parking space for said skinny broom. Now, gentlemen, this also does not mean that when you see a woman exhibiting this set of characteristics that she *is* a big B word any more than your aggression earns you the legendary lifetime label of a horse's bottom. None of us is exclusively one label—any more than we are one column label to the exclusion of the other three. However, behaviors brought on by stress have far greater emotions behind them and may appear out of the norm for someone, so they are quickly labeled for ease of future identification. The challenge is that these behavior descriptions, even in slang or in profiles, have been misused to describe who someone *is* versus what they *do*, particularly under stress.

When you see this label's behavior, particularly under the kind of exceptional stress I just described, what comes out is the negative version of otherwise highly prized and valued behaviors. Those negative traits look like aggression, control, bossiness, overly dominant directives or demands, and argumentative behavior. Just because someone is acting this way at the moment does not mean his or her total persona can be described by such behaviors. It means the person is under stress and they are doing what is as natural to them as breathing in an effort to mitigate or cope with said stress. No matter what words or labels you use, remember that it's about *behavior*, not someone's *personhood*. Unfortunately, we are still somewhat socialized to believe that an aggressive male is a jerk for a moment and an aggressive woman is a witch for a lifetime. I'm not sure where the fairness is in that labeling system." She smiled, as if in thought, and went on to say, "Well, fair or not fair, it does drive our lies and labels about behavior and helps us to see others as difficult, when instead their behavior is just difficult to handle at the moment. Besides, I've always been told that a 'fair' is something that comes to town once a year—and this ain't it.

"Labels allow us to simplify behavior and people assessments, but people aren't simple and neither is their behavior; nonetheless, we oversimplify and use name tags and colors and labels to categorize people instead of learning skills that enable us to read what they are showing us at the moment. Positive, middle-of-the-road, and negative sets of behaviors are exhibited by each personality preference. In the case of extroverted Commanders, their behaviors are outwardly visible and obvious, so they are one of the easiest to identify and label."

This would certainly explain why Cybil could never wrap her head around the premise that she had been told (and believed) she was broken, yet she didn't *feel* broken *all* the time. How could one be broken only part of the time? You either were or you weren't, right? She was able to pull off being fun, playful, and even soft many times, but when she wasn't, she got hit with a label that stung. Maybe her ability to deal with stress was broken, not her personality.

The trainer went on to talk about how Commanders were the ones also often labeled as type A. She explained that this, as with many of our labels, was not about the person, but rather something that the person had done; but it appeared there was more to this story. Before she could go on, half of Cybil's team shot quick glances and smirks in her direction. They had just talked about, or rather, made fun of, the laughable title of their next award. It was a joke, of course, but they had come up with "The Top Type A Team Member" award, as though they needed to reward workaholic tendencies. Were those really a good thing?

The trainer then described a study done in Toronto in the 1960s, designed to determine the effect of stress-related diseases and sickness. She added for emphasis, "In other words, they were studying people to learn their tolerance for stress and how much it took to *kill* them, yet here's the part you'll love. Each person in the study who died of a stress-related condition was promptly given a literal label, or toe tag, that identified the person as a part of the type A group. The type A group consisted of people who had *died* from being overstressed!" It was officially the last time Cybil would brag and laugh about being someone she now knew was likely to die from their inability to effectively cope with or mitigate stress. Oh, and the new award? Its nearly awarded "cute" label was completely off the table. Maybe they would now institute an award for the person who saw the least difficult people.

It occurred to Cybil just how often she used labels to describe the people around her. Earlier that morning she'd shared with her sister Simone that Philip was a type A. How many other labels had she been using for others that just didn't make sense or have any basis in truth for what they had come to mean. If the negative labels based on behaviors born out of our natural and authentic personalities were removed from the world's vocabulary, she wasn't sure how she would actually describe herself. Who was she, exactly? It was becoming a much more important question than what she did or how she acted.

"Because of their task-focused nature to lean toward task completion and getting it done, Commanders can be seen as uncaring, particularly when operating in their middle-of-the-road or negative mode. This doesn't mean they don't value people or feelings; it means if you're not on their list, you're not getting done." She then paused and smiled. "Figuratively or literally, I suppose." The trainer turned her focus to one of the members of the audience, "It also explains why they are so gifted at multitasking . . . much like Sherry here is listening to our course and surfing Twitter and Facebook at the same time. Tweet some good stuff about our class, okay?" She nodded and smiled and kept right on multitasking while Cybil looked on in horror.

The room laughed out loud at the pun and the teasing of a classmate they knew could handle it and welcomed the attention, and then eagerly looked around as the trainer asked, "Who in here has a high score in column A?"

Cybil held her hand up.

"There's more to explaining the differences between Commanders and all the rest, but let's spend some time covering the other quadrants first."

The trainer delved into the other personality trait set descriptions. She began, "Those who exhibit the behaviors found in the Organizer quadrant are the ones who most dislike being labeled. Keep in mind that *Organizer* here is the name of a quadrant, not a person, so let me tread lightly as we talk about those who scored the highest in column B."

She continued, "The people who are naturally dominant in this set of behaviors are often referred to as left-brained, partly because this is where these behavior traits reside in the brain. However, they are also usually linear and logical and maintain very clear frames of reference on what is right and wrong, black and white, good and bad. This applies to everything for those who have naturally developed a predominance of this set of behaviors. They have a right way to do the job, a right way to lead, a right way to raise children, a right way to be married, a right way to be a friend, and so on. Their motivation is to 'get it right,' and they usually do. They are also not typically very affectionate or expressive. In fact, a truly excited, overenthusiastic Organizer might look something like this."

The room just about fell apart as the trainer stood quite calmly in the front of the room, weight equally balanced on both feet, hands folded in front of her at the waist, and a smile that looked like she was straining to make it happen. She went on to say that Organizers (who, she reminded us again, hate to be labeled) rarely talk with their hands or move their hands from the position in which their elbows appear to be glued to their rib cage.

"What you'll find is that Organizers will act as if their arms are glued to the sides of their body, whereas more expressive and extroverted personality preferences will often unleash their arms to roam all over the space in front of them." The room erupted, and side conversations and giggles were seen at all tables, even those with self-admitted Organizer preferences present.

Cybil looked toward Jason, the CFO she had befriended over the years. He smiled and nodded, and then they both grinned widely, knowing this described *him*, and when the trainer asked how many in the room had a high column B score, his hand went up and stayed up for a long time period.

"Now I want to point out something. The Commanders, when I asked for a show of hands, stuck their hands in the air, finished the task and then quickly brought them down. The Organizers have left their hands up long enough for me to get an accurate count and the correct answer. You see, the question I asked was 'how many,' and because that question has a numerical answer, the Organizer preferences in the room caught the distinction and gave me time to count to ensure I got it right."

Cybil was starting to see the awareness, and she enjoyed watching Jason laugh at himself. He was a stickler for numbers, to be sure, and they'd had their share of discussions on this attribute of his. She now understood why his accurate observations on numbers, after only a moment of viewing a report, seemed like magic to her, but were natural to him.

"Let's talk more about their need for 'right-ness' and how it applies in the workplace. If you ever notice Organizers in a place where they are mentally struggling to make a decision, are acting very stubborn, and are vigilant about details to the point of perfectionism, then you are witnessing those who exhibit Organizer-dominant preferences under significant stress. The phrase 'analysis paralysis' comes from this preference's stressed state, where they need accurate details and more information, yet have an inherent pessimism and distrust of any details provided. The result is that they pull in like a turtle and refuse to make a decision about anything. They become paralyzed, or frozen, in a state of indecision until they perform further analysis."

She continued, "It can be painful to watch, but even more painful to experience, and can take some time to recover from. However, this type of thinking is a gift. Organizers are needed on each and every team you lead because this preference is the *only* preference that will exert the time, effort, energy, and patience to think through every single detail of a process or project to determine its viability."

She paused for emphasis before saying, "When an Organizer, or Organizer-dominant preference (to avoid overuse of the label here) speaks up and says, "This won't work 20 years from now," you should *listen!* You may think this person is being negative or a naysayer, but the truth is they are the usually *right*. The difference here is that Commanders will make a decision for the sake of getting a choice or action item off of their list and charge ahead, believing they can make it work. Organizers actually think it through. What events could we avoid if a Commander listened to his or her Organizer sidekick?"

The audience sat in silent consideration for a moment. The trainer then picked up again, "Let's move on to the next column and look at another set of behaviors. What is the label we give to high column C behaviors?"

The room was quick to answer in unison, "Relater." It wasn't just Cybil who seemed to be getting moments of epiphany from this information. Every one of her team members was engrossed in the words the trainer shared. What would happen, she wondered, if this type of effort continued in the halls at the office? Would they all be able to laugh at their own preferred behaviors? Would they understand why they worked for some but not for others? Would this be the key that erased the conflict she sometimes saw? Would it dissolve the lines some had drawn in the sand about whom they would work with? Time would tell, but she was hopeful.

The trainer moved on to describe the personality traits of the Relater behavior type. She said, "Those with Relater-dominant preferences are the most loyal, trustworthy, kind, caring, and nurturing individuals on the planet. These are the ones who will be your friend for a lifetime. They will always make time to listen regardless of what might be on their list, if they have one. Their gift is empathy, and they are motivated by the phrase 'get along.' In fact, these are the behaviors that women in our culture have been expected, in many cases, to play for decades. Even now, to some degree, women are expected to take care of the children, the household, and the husband and nurture everyone else's needs, while putting their own on hold or on the back burner. In fact, when this particular preference is faked, you get what I refer to as a possible member of the Red Hat Society. Are you familiar with this group of women?"

Make Difficult People Disappear

Cybil had to laugh as she recalled walking into a hotel when she and Dave were looking for wedding venues and seeing an entire group of ladies gathered for lunch—all dressed in red dresses and purple hats and shoes. They seemed to be quite a vocal group, but she wasn't sure she understood how these women were Relaters or faking anything.

"This is only anecdotal evidence, of course, but in my humble opinion, many of the Red Hat Society members, an organization designed for women 55 and over, are the very women who played, or faked, the Relater role for most of their lives. I say 'faked Relater' because of what you see in their behavior. My experience is that they are rather vocal and seemingly opinionated. This is not necessarily a bad thing, and they are fun to be around, but their behavior indicates that they have suppressed Commander traits for a number of years and only recently decided to let them out again.

If they were actually Commanders naturally and suppressed it, their Commander behavior is coming back out at the same level of development it had reached when they put it away. It would be kind of like holding a beach ball underwater for decades. Can you imagine holding a beach ball underwater for 40 or 50 years? If you did, after a while your arms would go numb, and certainly before that they would grow tired, but holding that beach ball down under the water would at some point become just something you did out of habit. Then, when you least expect it (perhaps when the children are grown or a spouse passes away), your eye is taken off of your proverbial ball and you let it go. The ball comes rushing up out of the water with a great big splash, and you are now somewhat at a loss for what to do with your free (but tired) hands that have let go of the ball. This is what I believe has happened for some of these women."

These predominantly Commander women have held that part of their persona underwater. Then, they let go of the need to suppress it for conscious or unconscious reasons and up comes the beach ball (in this case, their authentic *persona*), looking just like it did when it was suppressed years ago. If we liken the Commander behaviors to that ball, and a woman stuck those behaviors underwater when she was a little girl, they are going to come out appearing immature and underdeveloped. Thus, when these ladies speak up or speak out, it comes out sounding as if they could give a flip what you think about what they say or what they wear. One option is that it is merely a demonstration of underdeveloped and stressed Commander behaviors, not women who are inherently brazen or unnecessarily vocal. They are simply in an earlier stage of development in using these behaviors than the women who have been comfortable with using them all their lives.

"However, let's not focus only on women. Men can fall into the Relater category as well, and the same kind of suppression can happen for men who have a natural Relater tendency. Men have been expected to play the opposite role of what I just described for women. They have been often inaccurately placed in the boss, or Commander, role in much of our history. Sometimes, if that is not who they are, they fake it. When they are tired of faking it and their beach ball comes to the surface, they may decide to run out and buy an earring, hop on a Harley, and ride off into the sunset, never to be heard from again. Or they might retire in a quiet cottage away from anyone and anything that requires they be in charge, command anything, deal with conflict, or make a decision. Their need for isolation and for freedom from having to make decisions is so overdue, and they are so stressed from faking it for so long, that they appear to be having a midlife crisis."

"You see, at some point, no matter who you've learned to act like, we always end up going home, so to speak, to our natural and preferred style, one way or another. Part of what my role becomes is showing you how to go home before you wake up one day and find yourself forced to go there, running away from or running over everyone in your path to get to there. The goal is to keep your eye on the ball, but not to have it underwater. Make sense?"

Everyone seemed to have gotten it, and the trainer made eye contact with almost all of the participants before moving on.

"So, there's one personality preference we haven't talked about, and in some ways, discussing this one last is purposeful, as we want to be sure to give it significant attention. Who in here is a high column D scorer?"

There was an eruption of hands and cheers as 10 people in the class enthusiastically raised their hand. The trainer was woo-hooing, and it all just seemed a bit overdone to Cybil, but maybe she was energizing the class before lunch. The 10 people she just called on were certainly enthusiastic, but somehow Cybil was a teeny bit jealous of their freedom of expression and comfort in their willingness to celebrate their score. Or were they celebrating who they *were*?

"Entertainer preferences are the most enthusiastic, exuberant, charismatic, energetic, and fun-loving folks on the planet. They will talk to anyone, anytime, anywhere, and anyplace about anything, regardless of interest or ability to respond. They would converse with an inanimate object if one presented itself in the conversation. They tend to be excitable, emotional, and also to suffer from an attention span the length of a gnat's behind."

The trainer continued, "I've mentioned earlier that some personality types are likely to have a hard time with each other, and this is a prime example. The short attention span of Entertainers will particularly annoy the Organizer-dominant preferences when they are discussing strategic plans or sequential outlines. Entertainers, mind you, can't "spell" *outline*, much less think in that linear fashion. All of a sudden, Organizers will be diligently following their outlines, and Entertainers will mentally utter, 'Squirrel!' To an Organizer, it appears as if the Entertainer's brain has left the building!"

Cybil couldn't help but smile and wonder how many times that morning she had experienced a "squirrel moment." Staying focused and on track was hard for some people and that wisdom from the trainer certainly explained it. Cybil was now certain that she had used labels and made snap judgments by mistake. How often did she have an issue with people and simply label them "difficult" without investigating further or thinking about their needs?

As she drifted off in thought for a moment, she began to argue with herself. Everyone out there in her world seemed to be difficult at least sometimes. Cybil decided it couldn't possibly be all because of her perception. Was it okay to think *some* folks were difficult? Or were there really no difficult people out there at all, just well-intentioned people doing the best they could? She wasn't sure she bought that Pollyanna-like, positive-sounding idea, but some concept in the middle seemed plausible. If nothing else, these labels made more sense than others she had heard before. She was becoming more and more curious about the rest of the pieces and hoped they, would fall into place and make sense before the day was over.

For videos and more information that will enhance what you've learned in this chapter, go to: www.MakeDifficult PeopleDisappear.com.

Chapter 4

MAPS . . . Showing Where Others Can Go before Being Told

The class laughed out loud, and many couldn't stop for several minutes. The depiction of "squirrel!" from the movie *Up* was more than it seemed many of them could bear, and yet it was also frighteningly accurate.

Cybil began to think about her son Ben and his short attention span. She wondered if he, too, suffered from "squirrel moments." One minute he was talking about saving animals, another minute he was watching the cartoons, and the next he would be showing his dad the cool leaf he found on the ground at school. It was hard to keep track of his pinball-machine-like brain.

If what the trainer was saying was accurate, Cybil had a little Entertainer on her hands. She wondered if his teacher had this type of information. A few days earlier, Ben's teacher called and suggested that Ben be tested for ADD and that he possibly needed medication. Cybil's first thought was that this was a difficult teacher who wanted to medicate her son because she didn't know how to teach him. She realized now that she hadn't had any issues when Ben was in the first grade because that teacher had seemingly been a Commander, like Cybil, and they had easily seen eye to eye. This teacher was not cut from that cloth. Until today, their differences had led Cybil to believe the teacher was difficult.

It was becoming clear to her that Commander skills of saying "Next" and simply moving on was a gift, but that it was not the way everyone reacted. In fact, it was that "next" concept of Commanders that allowed her to sleep; and sleep had literally become a task on her list of things to do. She wasn't sure, but in the case of her son, she was going to defend his nonmedicated state pretty vehemently. It seemed that the lack of understanding of his personality was part of the problem, and she reminded herself to discuss this with the trainer during her one-on-one after the class. Could it really be a personality difference and a lack of understanding that kept much of the ADHD and ADD industry, and the medications tied to it, so incredibly profitable?

When Cybil turned her attention back to the trainer, she was addressing how to use the information from the session. She said, "So, here's part of the real value of this tool. Now that you know there are different personality preferences, which I daresay you already knew, the biggest question I get is, 'Now what?' How do you work with these differences in behavior without labeling those who are different as just plain wrong or insisting that they conform to your needs? This is what we tend to do. We click well with those who are similar or the same, but when most of us encounter people who are dramatically different, the tendency is to assume that they're not just different, but wrong, and, particularly, when stress is involved, purposely being difficult."

It seemed sad in a way that we often viewed others through a black-and-white prism, but what she said couldn't have been more true.

Cybil herself had struggled with this: for example, when Ben wanted to wear a different outfit or became distracted, when Dave showed lack of initiative, when her boss's black-and-white nature came to the fore, even when Simone's softer side seemed so natural. More than once she had thought to herself, *"Why can't they just do it right and get it?"* She was starting to realize that she was really thinking, *"Why can't they be just like me and do it the way I do?"* (or how she *would* have done it had she gotten herself into those situations)!

Cybil couldn't imagine being like Dave and not having a desire to do more or be more. She couldn't imagine not being able to focus, which her son seemed to struggle with. However, clearly, today her Entertainer kept coming out as she failed to focus regularly. *"Focus, Cybil, focus!"* she thought to herself. Why did she seem to have to say that so often?

"What you can do with this information is to build on what you know, raise your awareness, and then begin to add a bit of strategy and skill in your relationships. This isn't about manipulating relationships, but rather about molding how you talk with others to facilitate better understanding on their part and better relationships that involve less miscommunication. In fact, with this type of information, you can develop a road map for your relationships that tells you where they go in their behavior before you feel like telling them where to go *with* their behavior." The trainer giggled at her own imagery, but Cybil was laughing as well at the visual of having a map to point to when she wanted to tell someone where to go.

69

MAPS . . . Showing Where Others Can Go before Being Told

"I'll give you a prime example that has happened today about how this works. Who in here noticed that we asked for a show of hands of the high scoring column totals in each category, except one?" There were puzzled looks and then also several nods as one quiet participant slowly raised her hand. It was evident in looking at her that she was not completely comfortable pointing this out, but somehow it appeared she felt compelled to comply with the request by raising her hand. "You see, those of us who are not in the Relater high-scoring column didn't notice that we failed to ask for their show of hands earlier today. They likely noticed but as is also quite common, they didn't want to make a big deal out of it or draw attention to themselves, so they let it go. Who in here is a high scoring Column C individual?" There were about 25 hands that slowly raised to full extension. "What you'll also notice is that these people have raised their hands and then looked around the room to make sure all of their buddies got included as well. Relaters will look out for each other, but often not in a vocal sense. They will run from conflict and often avoiding saying how they really feel if they perceive the environment might put them on the spot or bring them unwanted attention." Many of the Relaters had facial expressions that indicated validation, and Cybil was surprised that even she hadn't noticed they'd been skipped. "So, now the question becomes, how do we avoid doing things just like this, skipping over team members, or habitually moving forward on a project, without ensuring that we really do have buy in or participation from even those team members who aren't likely going to demand they be involved unless you specifically

Make Difficult People Disappear

ask them? Keep in mind we typically do what works well for us and again, this is the behavior we often expect from others. You all have a high number of Commanders on the team and I suspect this happens more than you might realize. These Relaters, as well as all of your team members, have great value and contributions. Are you missing hearing it from them?" She paused only briefly but the point had been clearly made in a visual example that no handout could have helped them understand better.

"If we are always saying or doing things in the way that really works only for us, then we are doing those with whom we are communicating a disservice by expecting them to think and respond in the same way. It would be much like telling people to take a map and follow only your highlighted route to get to their destination, when there are at least three other routes that make more sense to them. Isn't the end result to get there? Isn't the end result of communication to get your message across and to be heard? Why do we expect that there is only one way to do that and that others haven't found a route that also works for them, one that might look and sound different yet still get them to the same destination? When those expectations are at play, it's no wonder workplaces, and lives, are rampant with miscommunications and unresolved differences that people begin to take personally. Let's take the differences between Commander and Relater behaviors as another prime example."

Fully focused, Cybil was eager to hear about the differences between her and her husband, though she was pretty sure she already knew them. He was laid back and she

71

wasn't. She was internally driven to learn, grow, and succeed, and he wasn't, or at least not in the same way Cybil felt she was (or maybe that was part of the problem).

"What do Commanders do when they are angry?" the trainer asked the class.

All were quick to chime in with comments that included yell, scream, throw things, stare intensely, get really bossy, become overly controlling, or act belligerent. It was a bit disconcerting, actually, to Cybil, as she did all those things when she was feeling out of control, but she hoped that didn't happen as often as it appeared based on the class's familiarity with these behaviors.

"In other words, they get really difficult to deal with, right?"

The class again was in agreement, and the Commanders were laughing as well. Cybil wasn't laughing, but instead was scanning the room to see how her own team members were reacting. Fortunately, no one was pointing or staring directly at her.

The trainer paused for a moment and then asked a simple question.

"Especially difficult for *whom* to deal with?"

The class didn't answer right away. Then the trainer persuaded Rick, one of the phone reps, to answer based on what she said was the look on his face. In the softest of whispers and almost only mouthing his response, he said, "Relaters."

"Exactly. And thank you, Rick, for sharing that insight. You are exactly right, and I appreciate you keeping us on target there. Commanders, when under stress, are perceived as being very difficult to deal with, particularly by the Relaters. Now others may think this as well, but Relaters really struggle, because they typically take these types of behaviors from the Commanders very personally. Mind you, Commanders may not personalize the stressed-out Relater behavior in the same way that Relaters tend to personalize angry or stressed Commanders, but they do struggle with negative Relater behaviors. It's just a different struggle or a different version of perceived difficulty. What do Relaters do when they are angry or under exceptional stress?"

The response this time was less enthusiastic and outspoken, because the Commanders really didn't know how to describe it, the Organizers were still thinking about the question, and the Entertainers had forgotten the question altogether. It really was comical to see all the traits in action in such living color. It was as if the map the trainer had referred to was starting to take on three dimensions. It was a neat analogy, actually, given the tool's acronym was CORE MAP. Until now, Cybil hadn't looked at it as a guide to behavior in quite that way. She could even envision this awareness and information diffusing a lot of misunderstandings in the days ahead.

In a few moments, the class began to speak up to answer the trainer's question. They shared things that Relaters may do under when under stress, such as becoming quiet, acting in a passive-aggressive manner, and whining, all of which were on the handout they were looking at. Not surprisingly, Rick remained quiet and seemed concerned that he might be called on again.

As the class continued to think about their answers, Cybil couldn't help but think about her husband. Every time they had an argument, she was the one who became red in the face. She would express all of her points until she was finished. It was almost as if there were items to be checked off of her list: Share opinion, have argument, check, check! Once that was done, she could move on and often did. It wasn't intended to be cold or disrespectful or inconsiderate of Dave's needs, but it just didn't make logical sense to her to share any more thoughts on the matter or discuss it further once she said what she needed to say. She assumed that he would also say what he needed to say at that moment, and if he said nothing, the assumption was he had nothing to share. However, it took him usually about three solid days to bring up the issue again. Even after she asked him what his opinion was or what he thought, giving him a full 30 seconds to respond, he would decline to engage in the conversation and would say he had nothing to share. Then he would come back to her three days later and ask if they could discuss the argument. She was always (or *almost* always) happy to discuss it again, but she just couldn't remember what the heck the argument was about and usually she had to play along for a while to catch up, because she had moved on to dozens of other items since then. She didn't understand the need to stew over something for so long, and it frustrated her. Couldn't Dave just share his input, participate in the fight, and be done with it, like she could? This was when she thought he was being the most difficult, yet maybe he was, in fact, just doing it differently.

Cybil was beginning to see how easy it was to miss the needs of others or to disregard their style and assume that everyone did things the same way. She also started to wonder just how many other areas of her life this might apply to—or, for that matter, how many others areas of work? There were a few customers she suspected of having Dave's same personality traits.

"You'll also notice a significant difference—again, not *difficulty*, but *difference*—in how the Relaters and Commanders deal with empathy. Who in here has ever had a bad day?"

It was a simple question, and the class wasn't sure how to answer, so she asked again and reminded them that lunch was coming soon, so she would keep the questions simpler. It was funny to see her in action and having such a well-honed command of the room. Time was flying, and no one was bored. They loved this trainer, and it showed.

Eventually, all had their hands raised to answer the question. Even though she was mentally multitasking, Cybil, too, had to admit to a bad day or two, often due to not being able to complete those items on her list.

"If you've ever had a bad day and you needed or wanted someone to listen to you in depth and with great focused attention *and* you are looking for someone to say 'awwwww' about your bad day, go to a Relater. Do not go to a Commander for this type of reaction, because to a Commander, empathy sounds a little bit like this: 'Wow. Sucks to be you!'"

They all fell apart at that point, and the Commanders were laughing the hardest. They couldn't help wondering:

How is it that Commanders can appear so coldhearted and yet be the very same folks often promoted into leadership and able to perform the role so successfully? Cybil believed she wasn't as "next" focused or task focused as the trainer described, and she hoped the trainer would address that.

"Now we're all laughing, but think of it this way. What happens if a Relater comes to a Commander and doesn't have this level of awareness and is looking for that 'awww' and expects to receive that, but doesn't? Do you think that Relater might think that Commander is difficult or cold?"

She continued with another example, "The same happens with Organizers and Entertainers. How frustrated are the Organizer-dominant preferences, since we know they are not just Organizers, when they encounter an Entertainer who can't "spell", figuratively of course, *outline*, much less follow one, or who wants to decorate the break room for birthdays when the Organizer doesn't really see the value in such fluff? Your polar opposites in the brain struggle the most with each other when one or both are under stress. Keep in mind, though, that we are describing *stressed-out behaviors*, not how these individuals operate all the time. We've all developed a strong set of coping skills and mechanisms, but when the stuff really hits the fan, how we cope will likely reflect who we naturally are—and our most dominant natural trait. Again, it is a behavior, usually brought on by stress, not a way of being for you or those other people. You all manage to work together beautifully until there's a major challenge or change or stressful event; and now that you understand some of the behaviors and some of the triggers, it would serve you well to look at how someone is behaving differently, yes?"

In response, the CFO of the company jumped in with a question. He asked, "How do you apply this to conversations with your colleagues?" Cybil was grateful to her friend for asking this question. It was the very question she had been thinking about. Jason was processing all the information and was curious to know how you applied this to employee conversations so that the right result was achieved in understanding. After the trainer teased him a bit about making sure that he had the right information, they both grinned, the class laughed, and she answered the question.

"Let's talk about takeaways here and how to apply this information in coaching, employee conversations, discipline, and even your client calls. The short answer is you merely want to remind yourself of what motivates the other person the most and then strategize a bit before you have the conversation. I'll give you an example. Have any of you ever bought a gift?"

The class half groaned and half chuckled as they remembered her remark about the upcoming lunch hour requiring easy questions.

"I know, I know, but go with me on this one. When you have gone out to buy a gift, the one you end up taking home with you is usually the one you liked the most, right?" There were many head nods in the room.

"Okay, makes sense. So who is the gift for?" She paused to let them answer.

MAPS . . . Showing Where Others Can Go before Being Told

"Whoever you're giving the gift to," answered the human resources director, and there was an almost audible "Duh!" that seemed to follow but was never spoken.

"Exactly. Yet, the gift you choose is the one YOU like. This usually means that it is something you'd like to have or that you think the recipient will like you more for getting. Our gift choices are more often about us then they are about the person for whom we're buying that gift, and the same is true of our communication effort with respect to the CORE attributes and our natural tendencies."

Had they been sitting next to each other it would have required only one lightbulb to fill the cartoon bubble above the heads of Cybil and the HR director. Cybil thought about her trip to Beth's Bakery with Ben. The sprinkles she had suggested as a gift (or, more accurately, a bribe) for Ben hadn't really been about Ben at all. They had been about *her* wanting to reclaim the feeling of, "I'm a good mom." She hadn't thought about what Ben really needed from her and how she could communicate that, with or without sprinkles; frankly, she wasn't even sure how to determine what he needed.

The trainer continued, "So, let's apply this to coaching in your office and the communication with your colleagues. This could be considered a gift from you the leader or peer, to the person receiving the coaching, but most of the time it's done to enable you to check off your list whatever is not getting done so that it *will* get done and you won't have to address it again, having done it right the first time.

She paused for emphasis and said, "Let's say that you have a team member who is a Relater. Let's use Jason as the example for this," and motioned toward Jason, the CFO, in the front row.

"And you, being a self-proclaimed Organizer, need to coach or counsel him about not talking with a customer in an unprofessional manner. Each CORE preference has needs, which are all different and when we go over your individual CORE MAP Profiles, I'll share these all with you, but for now, let me merely share with you some of the needs of the Organizer and the Relater. This will help you see how to structure a coaching conversation based on this information and will increase the effectiveness of those you conduct in the future." She proceeded to write out two flip charts, one for the needs of the Organizer and the other for the Relater.

Organizer Needs

- Details and facts
- Order and logic
- To be right

Relater Needs

- Reassurance
- Guidance
- Direction
- Stability

MAPS . . . Showing Where Others Can Go before Being Told

The trainer continued, "Keep in mind, these are not exhaustive lists of the needs of these preferences, but they will allow me to show you how to use this immediately after our class today. In fact, I want you to find the needs in the online CORE MAP Evaluation book, write out a plan for how you are going to address your most difficult employee challenge, and send it to me by Friday of this week."

She smiled as she doled out the homework, but no one questioned whether she was serious in her request. Cybil was glad to see her help with accountability. It wasn't something they had discussed before class, but Cybil struggled with it, as she just expected folks to get the things done that she assigned or that they knew needed to happen. Could that just be her Commander trait and strong motivation to get things done kicking in? Good grief, this stuff affected how she looked at everything! Cybil was just as eager to see how to use this in many different ways as Jason was interested in the right answer to his question.

The trainer returned to the question of how use the knowledge of personality distinctions in workplace conversation. She said, "So, Jason, you might address this employee naturally with a list of detailed behaviors that you overheard, words that he used with the customer that were unprofessional, and a bullet point list that you know is correct based on what you saw. You would have no problem sharing this information in a factual and detailed account of what you personally witnessed. You would then use logic to help him see the error of his ways—and perhaps even share possible consequences, something like 'up to and including termination if this behavior isn't corrected,' followed by the reminder that the company reputation is built on 'how customers see us, and in order for us to give the right impression, we have to do our jobs right.' Does that sound about right?"

"I think I may have to hire you to translate more of the messages in my head. That is nearly exactly what I would do," Jason shared, with a somewhat stunned look on his face.

"Happy to help," the trainer said with a smile. She then continued, "But the challenge with this is that though it is normal for us to do what is natural for us, the needs of the person you would be coaching are likely a bit different. You both need the behavior to change, so that can be your focal point, and the 'how you get there' needs to be based on his map, so to speak, not yours. The map he uses to guide his behavior includes the needs on this other chart. As a Relater, he needs stability, guidance, and direction. If you mention to him that he may be fired, he may never do it again, but he will also live in fear of losing his job and may just start looking for a new one based on that, because the instability of his position (or his *perception* of it) will stress him out. He also needs for you to tell him how to do it differently in the same circumstances (as opposed to just telling him what *not* to do). He needs guidance and then reassurance that you are a resource when he has questions. Your coaching conversation would have an outcome that is much closer to what you actually want if you ask him to confirm the facts, reassure him that he's right and that this is also the way you see it, and that you know that by working together, you can both resolve this issue and be better as a result. Rather than going logically down your list of offending behaviors, you ask him what he needs from you in order to change those behaviors. Walk him through what to do next time, step by step, allowing him to suggest improvements and confirming his choices, giving him the direction and the guidance he needs. Does that help?"

"More than I think you even realize," he shared in a brief moment of looking up from the notes he was taking as she talked. He looked very satisfied with her answer. Cybil knew that all the other participants were aware of who he was talking about, and they were eager to see him carry through. She was sure he would.

The trainer then continued, "Let's try a different example. Say you have a customer complaint and you want to send a representative out to fix the problem. If the representative is a Commander motivated by 'getting things done,' at a minimum (and other needs you'll get in your own sessions), then she will likely go out and do just that: fix the problem, or get it done, so to speak. She may or may not talk with the customer, make sure he was satisfied or build a relationship with him. You asked her to do a job and a task, and she did it. If what you want instead is for her to *salvage that customer relationship*, you want to make that the assignment, so she will not only fix the problem, but also *do* whatever it takes after that to complete the requested mission."

What she said made such perfect sense, and Cybil kept applying the information to her own team. She had folks in all four quadrants and struggled with each at times, though not as much with the Commanders, whose personalities were so similar to hers. One person in particular was great with customers but spent an inordinate amount of time with each one; this employee had recently given her a lot of pushback when she'd asked her to change. This employee had become a figurative member of most of her customers' families, and she thrived on the appreciation they gave her at the holidays and whenever she showed up.

Cybil had asked her to decrease the amount of time she spent with each customer—to socialize a bit less while still getting the job done. She appeared to be an off-the-chart Entertainer, which made her exceptionally good at sales, but also in need of a more socially oriented type of communication. Cybil didn't appreciate her efforts or the depth of the relationships she created with her customers. She didn't praise her for the time she spent or her above-average numbers. Instead, she asked her to change, hurry up, and do things differently . . . now. In hindsight, it was no wonder there hadn't been a significant improvement in the woman's time spent with customers. In fact, it appeared to have gotten worse, as she was now venting to her customers about how she might need to be looking for another job. Cybil was eager to try another approach with this team member soon.

"If you'll remember, Organizers, like our friend Jason here, are the ones most motivated by 'getting it right.' If you have a process that isn't working, ask them to find out what is wrong and then suggest a fix. Let them use their talent. If this is a discipline conversation, give them the decoder key for how to perform in the 'right' way so they know what to shoot for.

"Don't give Organizers some nebulous or vague direction like 'just go do it right' and expect them to interpret

83

MAPS . . . Showing Where Others Can Go before Being Told

right in the same way you do. They have their own version of right. Relaters are motivated by 'getting along' and are not the ones you want to argue with. Keep the conversation calm and factual and remind them of their value as people while pointing out the best way to get along well here at the office or with you.

"Keep Entertainers focused. Make your feedback lighthearted in some way—not sarcastic and not dire—and then share with them the consequences for their actions, but focus on the ways in which they can perform so that they get the appreciation that motivates them. Also, keep in mind that we have a dominant, a secondary, and a tertiary preference, so all of us understand each behavior, but we will almost always do what is most natural to us, or in some cases what is most heavily conditioned to feel natural, when under stress, and I would argue that saying, 'Can you see me in my office later today?' for a disciplinary conversation is stressful for most people. Would you agree? Are you starting to see how you can easily put this information into practice, how you can take with you what you are learning today and use it immediately?"

The CFO was still quickly taking notes and making what looked like diagrams of his whole team. Cybil admired his processing skills and had to laugh at the look on his face. You would have thought he was trying to solve the world's most difficult Sudoku puzzle, but the effort of learning this system seemed so worth it if she could keep folks from coming to her all day to talk about how much someone else had gotten on their nerves.

What was also starting to dawn on her was that all of those she led had tremendous value, and all of them had leadership potential. The trainer had mentioned earlier that in corporate environments such as this company's, Organizers and Commanders were often promoted into leadership. Thus the front line often consisted primarily of Relaters and Entertainers, and human resources employees seemed to have job security for the rest of their lives as a result. What a shame, she thought, that only two of the four types of behaviors were recognized as leaders. Didn't she consider Dave a leader of their family? Or did she? Didn't this also all apply to how Cybil and her husband communicated? She could remember one day asking Dave to take out the trash and wondering why it took so long. He'd made friends with the garbage haulers and talked with a neighbor. When he asked her to do something, she did the task and no more. It was how they had been operating for years and explained a lot. Neither behavior was right or wrong, but it was starting to seem like everything was relative to the perspective from which one was viewing it. Who on her team could take on a leadership role that she'd not given the chance because of this same kind of difference in perceptions of what worked and didn't in a leadership role?

The reality she was starting to see—in her own decisive, quick-to-find-the-logic, Commander fashion—was that all types or people or behavior sets were valuable and needed, and all had leadership potential. She was now wondering how many of each type she had on the team and whether there were gaps.

85

It was also right about that time that Gina, the human resources director with whom she shared the lightbulb moment earlier, was waving to get Cybil's attention. She waved and waved until Cybil looked in her direction. Gina then pointed enthusiastically to her phone. Apparently she had sent Cybil a text message. Cybil suddenly realized she hadn't checked her BlackBerry in hours. She was far too interested in the map being given to them to figure out where others went in their own behavior and the needs that drove them there, but the red light was blinking and she had to sift through many messages to find Gina's.

It said, "Where did you find this trainer? I need her contact info b/c we need her at the next SHRM conf."

It was another item to add to her to-do list, and she responded to tell Gina she'd let her know tomorrow. She also wanted to talk with Gina about the results of her own profile. She had always thought Gina was an Organizer type of preference, but the wild waving of arms and facial expressions and her excitement when she finally understood the concept earlier in the class gave Cybil the impression this was a closet Entertainer.

There were a lot of things being explained as a result of today, and they hadn't even had lunch yet.

Cybil was thinking about her coworkers as well as her husband, about her parents, her child, and so many things. As Cybil reflected for a moment on what she'd learned, she began to wonder in particular if her mom's old nickname for her had been born out of their misunderstood differences. Was it true that the first label Cybil had taken on was due to someone else's viewpoint . . . someone else's map? Her mom had always seemed to think something was very wrong with Cybil, but maybe she just didn't understand her mother's point of view. Maybe what Cybil had taken so personally all of her life, what she'd fueled and reinforced and crucified herself for by remembering the pain, was really more her doing than anyone else's. She wondered whether the message that she was "broken" was really the first inaccurate label that stuck like an extra-strength Post-it on her forehead for all to see and respond to. Somewhere she thought she knew the truth, but she'd been too easily swayed by external influences and had allowed too many other people to tell her who she was and where she was headed (and, in some cases, where to go). Some days she was too direct, bossy, or bitchy. Other days she was a great leader who developed people well and got a great deal done. It depended on the day, and there wasn't a lot of consistency.

Maybe that consistency came from within. Did she always like who she was? Did she even know who she was? Did she know where she was going and how she got there in her own leadership of her own behavior? Was she all that different and misunderstood by so many? Was anyone really all that different? Perhaps it was merely people with different preferences doing the best they could to communicate what they knew in the only way they knew how. Everyone had their own map, and maybe she was closer to discovering who she was than she thought. It seemed that the disconnect, the significant gap, between her current reality and what was truly known was closing. It felt a little scary, but it was also exhilarating.

This class was a rare opportunity for self-development, and Cybil made a mental note to ask about expanding the numbers of folks who participated in the comprehensive online CORE profile. As she understood it, the online profile showed much more in-depth information and provided for more awareness and self-management and she was easily starting to see justification to make the investment in even more team members having access to this kind of "Map."

For videos and more information that will enhance what you've learned in this chapter, go to: www.MakeDifficult PeopleDisappear.com.

Chapter 5

PRAISE . . . without Pom-Poms
Unless That's What They Need

The class broke for lunch, and Cybil did something different. She ate in the break room with some of her colleagues and team members. She would normally hibernate in her office and get more work done.

She'd never really thought about her actions, but something that was said in the class made her wonder whether eating alone sent a message different than the one she intended. She really enjoyed working with most members of the team and thought this might be a great way to share that subtle message.

As she looked around the break room, she noted the differences among other the leaders and their teams. Many of the team members seemed to have their hands raised when the trainer called for Entertainers and Relaters. Much of the front line was in fact in those two categories. On the other hand, her colleagues and fellow leaders seemed to fall more into the Organizer and Commander categories.

The trainer spoke about the connection between personality and leadership, and now she was seeing it in vivid technicolor. She wasn't convinced that all of her fellow leaders were authentic Commanders or Organizers, but she was starting to realize that the culture of the organization had encouraged them to act as if these were their authentic dominant traits in order to get promoted. After all, Commanders got it done and Organizers got it right, which were great assets for leadership. But were they doing the organization a disservice by glossing over the value of those Entertainer and Relater traits at a leadership level? Did the fact that the leaders communicate such task-focused behavior (versus the front line's more people-focused behavior) create some of the problems they were experiencing? If so, that was something worth changing.

Cybil hoped that by eating with the team, she was possibly making headway in changing the team dynamic. She wanted to show those she felt she had the privilege of leading that people mattered and that she valued them as team members. She wasn't sure they would understand her sacrifice: She could have zipped through so many e-mails in an hour's time! Of course, it was considered a sacrifice only by the Commander side of her, which needed to get more done. And was it her inner Entertainer who needed someone to appreciate what she was giving up? For a fleeting moment she also wondered if it was her Entertainer trait set that caused her to feel as if some days she should wear pom-poms permanently attached to her hips to get their attention. At least the visual was humorous.

She wanted a secret decoder key that would unlock the secrets to people's behaviors, and it didn't even have to be all that secret. After the morning session, Cybil felt that the solution to making the difficulty on her team disappear was becoming much clearer. She made a mental note to ask the trainer about the lists of needs and the other tools that could be effectively put to use.

The banter in the break room was comical. There was the discussion of key clients and their possible preferences. There were various conversations about wives, husbands, and children—stories that would have seemed out of context at any other time. There was quite a pleasant buzz in the office today. The key question on Cybil's mind was what would happen next. The mood in the office was great during the learning experience, but would they all know what to do with the knowledge when the class was over? That remained to be seen, but she was reasonably confident it would.

As the cleanup of Tupperware and homemade lunches began, (for those who didn't like the pizza they brought in) Cybil noticed her boss in the doorway. It suddenly hit her like a two-by-four that he had been waiting in his office for their rescheduled meeting. She immediately stood up and began to move quickly and precisely. The look on her face was one of "I'm coming right now" mixed with gentle remorse. She caught his eye again, and what she saw surprised her. His face broke into a slight smile as he mouthed the words, "We'll handle it later." With that, he disappeared from view. There was no sign of irritation or anger, and Cybil couldn't figure out why he seemed so relaxed.

She had clearly forgotten about their meeting and felt horrible. She continued to move quickly, intending to follow him down the hall to explain why she had forgotten. At the doorway, she almost ran over one of her team members who seemed to appear out of nowhere. Tim was her most difficult team member, and she had no idea where he had come from or why she hadn't seen him standing behind her boss.

93

She kept moving as she started to say she had to go, but the look on his face told her to stay. She glanced down the hall to find her boss, but he was already out of sight.

Tim was someone she struggled to lead and struggled to read. She wasn't sure what to make of his behavior most of the time. He lacked follow-through skills, yet was comfortable sharing stories. He blew up when she called him on his lack of adherence to any number of deadlines, and most of the time he seemed either very flighty or very intense. There was no middle ground with Tim. He either spread contagious charisma all over the office or appeared so overwhelmed and frustrated that he took the whole office down with him. It was like being on a roller-coaster ride, but she didn't remember buying the ticket.

He had a tough time finishing his own work, but was always happy to lend a hand on any matter that didn't involve one of the many projects he was responsible for. He even seemed to create more work for himself and then used his new suggestions as an excuse not to complete his original assignments.

If she pushed Tim on a deadline, he blew his top in front of anyone who would listen. Yet if she wanted to brainstorm with him, he was Johnny-on-the-spot. Quite candidly, she admired his insights. However, she'd had to pull back on the projects she discussed with him, because he had enough on his plate with his regular work and she didn't want to distract him. It was frustrating. Tim was brilliant, but seriously lacked focus. As she saw the look on his face, she wondered what he thought of the class and what he wanted from her now.

He continued to just stand there looking sheepishly in her direction but evading real eye contact. He had her attention, and she motioned to herself as if to say, "Are you looking for me?" He nodded slowly in response.

"What's up?" she said casually.

"Can we talk for a minute?"

"Sure, come into my office. Are you okay?" Something seemed to be really bothering him, and she wasn't sure what it was this time. Tim said he had a short fuse for drama, but he seemed to create it and thrive on it more often than Cybil was comfortable with. He reminded her of Charles Schulz's Pigpen character, but instead of a cloud of dirt, a cloud of drama followed him around.

"This trainer is driving me crazy. She is too animated and too fluffy and keeps making generalizations about me that just aren't true."

"Okay, what is she saying that's bothering you?"

"She's just too all over the place, and the people at my table keep talking. I've asked them to stop, and they won't. Do you mind if I go back to my desk and focus on the things that are really important?"

Cybil smiled inside as she realized what was happening. Tim was operating in his Organizer mode today. The look on his face and his comments struck her as a clear indication that he was not feeling very comfortable with being labeled and also was not enjoying the chatter of the off-the-chart Entertainers sitting at his table in class. His Organizer mode also explained other things, such as the very introverted style with which he had gotten her attention and why he was not comfortable talking directly about how he felt.

Then again, perhaps his Commander need for control had kicked in. Maybe he was more frustrated by the fact that the folks he was sitting with hadn't done what he'd asked.

Cybil responded, "I understand, and yet I think this *is* really important work. What if you move your seat to my table or another table and we'll make time to talk about how you might be able to use this information with some of your colleagues tomorrow morning when we're both in early?"

"I don't see how I can use it, at least not in a way that doesn't feel like manipulation. It would be as if I am changing who I am to fit the needs of these other silly people." It was a rather condescending remark, but this part of Tim she was used to.

There were many occasions in which she thought his behavior seemed a bit arrogant, yet she knew he meant well. He was a brilliant accounts payable rep and great at making sure things were accurately recorded and kept up to date. He was even brilliant with obscure computer issues that the company's own IT department couldn't seem to diagnose. He did struggle to pay vendors on time, but it was usually because someone didn't give him the right paperwork or because some other project that he'd created for the betterment of the organization got in his way.

She was never able to figure out whether Tim was more analytical or more of a control freak. Though now it seemed to be getting clearer and she thought she would try something different this time. He begrudgingly agreed to meet her the following morning, but still didn't look happy.

"Could you also do me a favor?" she began with one eyebrow raised for impact. "I'm sure you know that we've invested time and money into this program, and I would like to have you evaluate the course."

The look on his face revealed his interest. She could see that by giving him something to control and a way to notate all the ways in which he felt the trainer was doing it wrong, her strategy was working.

Cybil continued, "Can you look for all the ways in which we might measure the effectiveness and outcomes of this course and the information we learn today? Could you also put that in a spreadsheet with each key area in a separate column and the names of all the team members on the left column?" There was a continued spark of interest in his eyes.

"Would it be all right if I added time frames to those metrics, like one week, 30 days, and 90 days? That might allow us to correlate over time the return on investment from the program."

"That would be ideal, and I would sure appreciate that. I know it will be hard to be a participant and an evaluator in the same course, but I think that information would be very valuable to us going forward. Putting some logic behind these feelings would also help those on the team who lean toward the Organizer preference. There's not a rush on it, but logically the sooner after the class you complete it, the fresher the information will be. Does that sound right to you?"

Tim nodded, and Cybil was excited to see how easy it was to meet the needs of her newly discovered Organizer-dominant (with Commander a close second) team member. Maybe he wasn't difficult, but simply different in his approach to work and in need of something different from Cybil.

"In fact, if you shared it with me sometime next week, that would be completely fine." She knew that he would take his time and be diligent about it, making sure to get it right, and that it might be a week or more before she saw the document. She also knew that this would give his linear, logical, and naturally pessimistic outlook something to focus on. But she had also gotten Tim to agree that it was logical to turn it in soon after class, so maybe this time it would be different. She was beginning to see that although he operated well under pressure, he worked best when the pressure was of his own making.

It was a start, and Tim left her office with a spring in his step, saying, "Okay, let me find a new place to sit so I can focus, and I'll see you in there."

She almost said aloud, "What just happened here?" and then caught herself and realized she, too, needed to be heading in the direction of the class.

■ ■ ■

After lunch, the whole class was put into groups based on their highest-scoring column on the CORE Snapshot™ document they had all filled out in the morning portion of class. They were then asked to assign a leader and come to a consensus on the group's four most common pet peeves, or things that bugged them in general, as well as a short list of their favorite things to do and the group's preferred communication style. Of course, the Commanders finished their lists first, and their pet peeves far exceeded four.

The trainer shared the reality of Commander behaviors under slight stress and reminded the group of their tendency to find fault with things that were inefficient or got in the way of the results they craved. The pet peeves they listed included inefficiency, people who didn't get it, and having to repeat themselves. It was clear that essentially anyone outside of the Commander group seemed to embody the behaviors that appeared on their pet peeve list, and the entire classroom laughed out loud at this realization.

The Commanders finished first because of their repetitive need to compete and win. The praise for that achievement came from an internal source in their own head, but also because of their natural tendency to get things done and move on to the next item. Cybil wondered how often she disregarded a relationship opportunity for the sake of moving to the next thing or failed to notice the internal praise she gave herself for moving so quickly through her list.

The list of items from the Organizer group was equally revealing, as was the way they had written the list on their flip chart. Each item was in sequential order of importance, perfectly lined up and numbered in a neat and tidy fashion. They were more quiet and considerate when they shared their pet peeves, and their favorite things to do were those items that could be done individually versus with a group.

Jason, the CFO, had been chosen as the leader for the Organizers, and he guided the group with precision to come up with the answers that precisely matched the instructions given. When the trainer asked for their preferred communication style, it was clear there had been a struggle to come up with this answer. Team members with

99

their second highest scores in the Relater column craved face-to-face communication to build relationships and to get things right in interpreting the communication, whereas those with high Commander scores as their secondarily dominant preference preferred to communicate via e-mail for its efficiency and ability to get all their thoughts out succinctly and correctly without interruption. They couldn't decide between the two answers, and in order to most precisely follow the instructions, they took a vote to find the majority winner.

Cybil wondered how often she had shared instructions with a colleague or teammate that had lacked clarity and sounded a bit more like, "Oh, just get that done," leaving those with the Organizer-dominant preference faced with the need to read her mind to figure out how to accomplish that particular task.

The Relater group members were the quietest of all, and each member of the team seemed far less intense than members of the Commander or Organizer group. It also was glaringly obvious that most of the Relater team members were on the front line and without management titles. It was clear that the company's leadership team adhered to the common practice of promoting into management only those with Commander or Organizer traits.

The Relater group seemed to make the exercise a truly collaborative effort. They all rallied around their ideas and came to the consensus that their pet peeves were rudeness, people who created conflict, and constant change. Most of their pet peeves were traits that Commanders found as natural as breathing.

Cybil made several mental notes and began to wonder whether there was room for a softer approach on the leadership team, but also whether the Relaters had what it took to come to the leadership table with their own opinions, insights, and ideas without feeling run over by the vocal members of the rest of the leadership team.

The trainer then shared a story that helped Cybil clarify this idea into an action item. "One thing that is important to recognize about Relaters, as you have no doubt begun to see in their list of items and choices, is that they are stronger than most people give them credit for. They have definite leadership capabilities. They may not come across as intense and may not jump in to push someone out of the way, figuratively, of course, like a Commander might, but they have a natural gift that others have to work on to demonstrate."

She paused to be sure everyone was listening, and then continued, "Let me give you an example. At one time I reported to a gentleman by the name of John, who was the leader of our entire training team. He was a soft-spoken man and had a deeply Southern accent. Most of the time you would see him in his office, minding his own business, making himself the true example of an open-door policy if you needed him. However, when you needed him and walked in the door of his office, saying something like, 'Gotta sec?' here's what would happen: John's computer sat on the back credenza of his office, which allowed him to look out the window to think, and he would hit a key on his computer to make it go to the screen saver. He would then wheel around in his chair, hit the mute button on his phone, and gather up all the papers on his desk, only to tuck them into a folder literally labeled 'Clear Desk.' Then he would sidle up to his desk, clasp his hands in front of him on the desk surface and say, 'Why, yes ma'am, I do, come right on in. What can I do you for?' The entire process took about two minutes. The first time you bothered him for a simple or silly question, you realized this was not the man you approached to ask a question like, 'Hey, do you have a pencil I can borrow?'"

She continued, "What I learned, though, was that this *was* the man you went to if you really needed to talk. And in later years, I realized just what he did. The man didn't do anything to actually help, but he listened intently and asked great questions. You left his office having all the solutions you needed, *and* you came up with all the answers on your own. It was as if he taught you how to think by listening to what you thought."

After finishing the story, the trainer waited to let the information resonate with audience. She then asked, "How often do you listen intently to the needs of others so that you can truly help them become better leaders and learn how to resolve their own challenges? This is a natural gift of Relaters and a trait sometimes overlooked in a corporate setting. Would you agree?"

For a moment, there was the sound of silence. It was crystal clear as she shared the story that the Commander group seemed to have a newfound respect for the Relater team. The Relaters nearly glowed in the very spots where they stood. It was as if they were being given credit for what many called "weak" behavior. There were going to be some changes in the office after this class, and Cybil was excited at the prospect of keeping up the momentum.

The last group to share their input was the Entertainer team. It seemed fitting, because they held the spotlight longer than the others and were full of life and energy in their presentation. It appeared to be more of a dog-and-pony show than a mere sharing of what was on their list. They had written their list in multiple colors, and everyone had put their own version of input on the chart, written in different directions, handwritings, and styles.

The reaction from the crowd was mixed. The Organizers were visibly straining and seemed to frown in an effort to follow along, but couldn't suppress a smile when one of the Entertainers shared that his favorite thing to do was to watch an Organizer struggle with being able to juggle multiple topics in any one conversation. They were fun and not being difficult on purpose. Energy and charisma is what they brought most naturally to any team. Cybil couldn't argue with the value of having a little more fun around here. She even laughed when the entire Entertainer team high-fived each other at the end of their presentation. The whole room did.

There was so much more to this tool and the personality preferences than Cybil had imagined, and she couldn't help but apply each of them to her own family. Ben was so clearly an Entertainer, and her husband was the Relater. It seemed to fit and yet also made her look like the Big Bad Wolf at times. She wondered if the same was true for Simone and Philip. She could easily envision Philip in the

Commander group with her, while Simone would be a Relater.

As they returned to their seats, Gina, the HR director, walked up to Cybil and asked what she thought.

Cybil replied, "It's amazing, actually, and something that would certainly be good to know when we are conducting promotions and transfers to other teams. Plus, I want to know more about how to apply this information in recognition efforts. What about you?"

"I *love* it! This is so much fun." And then she almost visibly composed herself to shift her focus to the business application. "I'm also thinking this might be a good way to benchmark people we hire to determine more accurately whether those who are merely great in the interview process have the skills that are most natural to them to become star performers on the job. Isn't that something she had mentioned she would help us determine?"

Cybil nodded as Gina continued, "I could see this analysis as a highly valuable piece as long as we make sure it isn't a critical part of our hiring process. The EEOC guideline states that information of this kind can consume no more than 30 percent of the hiring decision, so we'd have to be careful not to cross that line."

Cybil agreed and felt it was doable, but was in a completely different train of thought in her own mind. She wondered whether Gina actually knew how much Entertainer was a part of her natural skill set. She was starting to see now that she was acting as if she were an Organizer, and Cybil wondered whether it took as much energy to act that way all the time, as she assumed it must. It seemed to be very similar to her own efforts of trying to be more of that Relater when her natural state was a Commander. She reminded herself to ask the trainer about it later.

They all returned to their seats and, almost as if the trainer had overheard Cybil and Gina's conversation, she asked the question "Okay, so now what? How do you apply this new knowledge you have to other aspects of the leadership role you have with colleagues, customers, and employees? Let's take a look.

"As leaders of yourselves and those you work with, there are some key skills and behaviors you'll use on an almost daily basis: coaching, motivation, and, hopefully, recognition of those performing their jobs well. We've already talked about coaching a bit and ensuring that your directions for development or actions for improvement actually encourage people to achieve your truly desired outcomes. Now let's take a look at recognition. Who in here likes to receive recognition for a job well done?"

It no longer seemed to matter to anyone in the classroom who held which titles. The trainer had attached value to each and every behavior type and preference and, as a result, had also given participants permission to just be themselves and share their needs openly. This was the type of freedom that Cybil looked forward to continuing after class. Maybe after this training, unlike many others, she and those in this class wouldn't go right back to doing what they had always done.

The Entertainers, of course, all had their hands held high, with a couple of them using both hands, eliciting just the giggles and attention they were looking for. This time, though, no one seemed to mind or take it personally. It was just how they needed to do things.

Others raised their hands, but very few Commanders raised their hands to indicate they liked to receive recognition. The trainer pointed out this difference.

"So, one or two of the Entertainers would like some recognition. Shocking!" she said, with a dose of sarcasm and a very obvious, but genuine, smile.

She continued, "What is also interesting is that most of the Commanders do *not* have their hands up, and I want you to pay attention to this observation. You see, Commanders are far more intrinsically motivated. They often move at such a fast pace that they forget what they are being recognized for by the time we get around to pointing out their achievement. It can be a downfall for Commanders in that they don't spend a great deal of time recognizing their own accomplishments and thus feel little or no need to spend time on it for others, either."

People looked around the room, nodding in agreement as the trainer continued, "Commanders, pay attention to the reality that almost every other preference in the room is looking for some kind of recognition. However, let's all pay attention to the fact that everyone needs recognition in different ways, even differently than your preferences would suggest. In fact, there are four different kinds of recognition. They are Public, Private, Tangible, and Intangible."

She went through the explanation of each, and some of it surprised Cybil. She had never heard recognition explained this way, but it certainly made sense. Some folks

Make Difficult People Disappear

prefer to have a tangible item in their hand or on their wall to show their achievements and recognition. Others just want a kind word or two from someone whose opinion they value. It was almost intuitive, but the explanation gave Cybil more of that "cheat sheet" she needed to put the information to use.

They all laughed heartily at one of the trainer's examples when she explained how to recognize people as combinations of the four types. She shared first that everyone was usually a combination of two out of the four types: Public Tangible, Private Intangible, and so on.

One of her examples was of a former employee of hers when she led a team of trainers in a corporate role. She had given each team member a PayDay candy bar along with their paychecks as a simple and easy way of saying a special thanks to the team for their efforts. She admitted she didn't think about the four types of recognition then and that, if she had, what she saw one team member do with the candy bar would have made much more sense.

She explained that he literally placed the candy bar on his desk in front of his computer and left it there for weeks. When people walked by his desk and said, "Hey, man, aren't you going to eat that?" he responded, "No way, that was a gift and reminds me of what a good job I do."

He was clearly public and tangible, but it isn't always so easy to tell. After all, not everyone would let a candy bar fossilize on their desk or find that valuable. The trainer then asked how people could tell which person is which type. One of Commanders blurted out, seemingly in spite of himself, "Ask them." The trainer was quick to point out that none of us had likely sat around contemplating if we were public or private, tangible or intangible in our recognition needs prior to this class.

She suggested, "Instead of asking, watch what people do for each other and for themselves, and that will give you great insight into their recognition style." To illustrate the power of observation, she offered an example of a leader with a big office who had hung on his wall every single plaque, certificate, and ribbon he'd won since the second grade—including the sixth-place ribbon from his middle school graduation potato sack race! She asked the class which type he might be, and they resoundingly answered, "Public tangible."

She continued, "You can test out a few things and see if the motivation from such positive reinforcement continues, but then I also want you to consider the differences that their personality preferences will make. Organizers, for example, because they are more introverted, largely prefer private recognition, but that doesn't mean that if you say, 'Hey, Bob, you did a great job on that project yesterday,' that you're going to capture their interest. In fact, a highly developed and dominant Organizer preference might dismiss these words because they are not specific enough. Remember the need for details earlier on the flip chart? What you want to say instead is something that points out details and specific tasks done correctly by that person. For example, 'Hey, Bob, I really appreciate the fact that you spent more than 10 hours putting together the spreadsheets for our consumer preference analysis. You did a great job in determining which preferences were critical to point out and highlighting those areas in which we are missing the mark. It really provided a great deal of value to the project and gave us a clear direction.'"

As the example sunk in with the audience, she continued, "Focused and detailed feedback will encourage the Organizer to repeat those behaviors in order to receive that kind of recognition again. A less specific version of recognition will likely give them reason to suspect your words are merely lip service. Does that make sense?"

Did it ever! Cybil watched and participated as the trainer asked each participant to list their team members and attempt to determine which two types of recognition they would find most valuable. The point was not lost on Cybil that, here again, much as in communicating a message, the point of sharing recognition is to thank the person in a way that they understand and can then repeat if they choose. It isn't about just being able to check off of your list "Gave recognition." It isn't always about whipping out the pom-poms, having a ticker-tape parade, or awarding a big trophy. On many occasions in the past, Cybil found herself ignoring these simple recognition guidelines, both with her team at work and with Ben and Dave at home. She seemed to give attention or recognition because she knew they needed it. The problem was, that kind of recognition was about *her* checking it off of her mental list versus what others needed and would find most valuable.

She knew that Ben would really prefer more spontaneous and playful recognition, while Dave would prefer that she spend quiet time with him, doing nothing more than having a conversation about his day and quietly telling him how much she appreciated whatever he had done or how he had made her feel.

What Cybil did instead was to *schedule* time with Ben and tell him that she would be home at 6:00 PM and would have fun with him then. With Dave, she would always end up dominating the conversation with stories about *her* day and how they might be helpful to him should he find himself in similar situations in an office environment at some point down the road. She didn't give him reassurance, which she knew he needed, and she didn't recognize his efforts in a private fashion. Instead, she would talk about him at parties or other events and publicly recognize him because that is what *she* preferred. She hadn't realized this bothered him until he told her one night that public displays of appreciation embarrassed him.

Her husband wasn't the type to tell her that he needed some time that was all about *him*—or perhaps about the two of them. Instead, he assumed that she needed to vent more than he did, and he put his needs after hers. There was only one time that he pointed this out to her, and, despite her best efforts, she found herself having to focus considerably to keep the conversation on his feelings versus her thoughts about how he could fix his behaviors.

She was beginning to see that there wasn't anything *wrong* with his behaviors and that they were, in fact, just radically different from hers. However, she also knew deep down that what he needed wasn't actually all that radically different. He just wanted to be loved, and he needed Cybil to show him that she did love him. Do the Entertainers always want gifts or Words of Affirmation[1] because it is a public form of appreciation and they are extroverts? Do the Relaters want primarily acts of service and quality time because of their desire to focus on people and helping them? She wasn't sure, but she was clearly beginning to see there was more to a relationship than just what *she* wanted.

She reminded herself to ask her coworker Jason about the diagrams he was drawing in class. She also promised herself not to act as if she had pom-poms attached to her body when he told her he had it all figured out and provided a well-documented cheat sheet. She'd find another way, one more easily understood by him, to show her appreciation for his efforts.

For videos and more information that will enhance what you've learned in this chapter, go to: www.MakeDifficult PeopleDisappear.com.

---

[1] Words of Affirmation is one of the five love languages featured in Gary Chapman's book, *The 5 Love Languages: The Secret to Love That Lasts* (Chicago: Northfield Publishing, 2010).

PRAISE . . . without Pom-Poms Unless That's What They Need

Chapter 6

CLUES . . . That You Can Finally Hear

After their discussion of recognition styles and a bit of practice on how to share recognition differently with different team members, they took a break. This time Cybil didn't even go to her office. She spent time talking with her colleagues and connecting, using her newfound knowledge. She wanted to share her more people-focused behavior rather than merely her task-oriented drive. She also confirmed with the trainer that they would be meeting a half hour after the class to go over her individual in-depth profile results.

When the group came back from break, the last section of the day's class was spent on driving home the skills needed to use this information. The trainer had them write scripts for each personality preference, including what they had learned that day about recognition, communication, coaching, and strategies for addressing each personality preference, even when they were outside the workplace.

The trainer also had them match up common phrases and words that appealed more to one preference than another.

The Relaters connected "Get to the point" and "Avoid social chitchat at first" with Commanders, as well as "Make an appointment" and "Keep information sharing within the scheduled time whenever possible." The Organizers practiced acknowledging the creative ideas of their Entertainer colleagues, realizing that it would go a long way to say things like, "That might be a great idea!" with some enthusiasm, while avoiding commitment to calling it the right idea.

Relaters enjoyed hearing "I appreciate your contributions" and "Thank you for your help." Organizers responded well to "Can you explain how that process works?" and "What's the best way to get this right?"

People still had to be true to themselves in using the phrases they chose. The goal was to make an effort to demonstrate an understanding and appreciation for the other preferences. No one can operate effectively without the partnership and influence of the other types. Even the Commanders and Entertainers were writing scripts. Those made by the Commanders were shorter, and the ones made by the Entertainers were rendered in colored markers with arrows and colored dots on the left, but there was more than one way to do the assignment. As they did in this case and most of the time, the different methods all led to similar outcomes.

They role-played coaching with a manager, an employee, and an observer, and even tossed a ball around the room, with the idea that whoever caught it had to share one thing he or she had learned that day. Responses from the audience ranged from "I learned how to work with my boss" to "I learned how to sell to that customer who's been dodging me" to "I learned how to save my marriage." It had been a powerful day, and Cybil was so proud of all of their efforts. She was also grateful to the trainer for being authentic in sharing herself and focusing on each preference they needed to learn. It was so much more than she had expected, and she couldn't wait to learn more about her own profile. She planned to use all of this information at home and at work, much as she had already begun to do that day. It had taken some conscious thought, but as the trainer pointed out in her closing comments, "Leadership and life do not go well when you carry them out on autopilot."

Cybil decided that the first step in changing her interactions with the people around her would be communication. Being consciously aware of how you say things or speak to someone else isn't a bad thing, and she saw it as beneficial to making sure you were understood and didn't misinterpret others. This awareness was the key she had been looking for to elevate her communication and leadership skills and to reduce the instances of seeing so many others as difficult. She hadn't been looking for a new perspective on the difficult people in her life, but now saw that her quick judgments and misinterpretations of the needs of others were the real catalyst to seeing so much difficulty in others or difficult people.

The reality is that people really are just different. Not only that, but she added to the difficulty by assuming everyone acted or knew how to act just like she did and was motivated by the same things. If a little practice and conscious effort were really all it took to no longer have to deal with so much conflict or misunderstanding in the office, she was willing to immediately hit the off switch on her autopilot mechanism.

When class ended, the nonmanagement team members immediately packed up their belongings and began their mass exodus. The dominant Commander and Organizer preferences on the management team retreated to their offices to handle some last-minute e-mails and get a few things done. Cybil noticed it all, and she wasn't surprised by the behavior because now she had a better understanding of it. She stopped by her boss's office to share some of the good news and to follow up on the meeting that she'd missed at lunch and his unexplained reaction to her oversight. She was surprised to find him gone for the day and asked his assistant about it.

"Hi, Cybil. He's actually left for the day. He always leaves early on Tuesdays for his son's Little League game. Do you want to leave a message?"

She nearly had to pick herself up off the floor. She had worked with this man for more than five years and had never noticed that he left early on Tuesdays; she didn't even know he had a son who played Little League. She vaguely remembered seeing pictures, but didn't recall many details. She had been contemplating how to casually tell her boss that he might have benefited from this class in more ways than one and that he might want to treat those he led a little differently as a result of what they learned.

Instead, it dawned on her that her boss was perhaps more well-rounded and developed than she thought. He made the time for what was important to him, and his assistant worshiped the ground he walked on, yet Cybil was the one who was in the dark. Was *she* the one with difficult behavior that he was effectively leading? She enjoyed working with him, but noticed that he was very task-focused with her and didn't mention any family issues. In fact, she'd been afraid to tell him about Ben's bake sale and the cookie emergency, but for some reason she now thought he might have understood better than she'd imagined.

Maybe her boss was leading her in the way she demonstrated she needed to be led. It was all business all the time and no play, much less personal sharing. She was work-focused around him, and he was behaving the same way in response. If Cybil had to guess, her boss was an Organizer preference who wanted things done right, but he also treated the people he worked with using respect, dignity, and a bit of warmth. Different people saw different sides of him. His assistant had seen that warm Relater side more than Cybil had. Cybil now realized that his Relater side also accounted for the strong loyalty to his son and his family that she learned about today.

Cybil thanked his assistant and headed back to her office wondering how many other people she had been unwittingly "training" how to treat her by the demonstration her own behavior.

■ ■ ■

The trainer was headed down the hall toward her office from the direction of the training class and looked happy to see Cybil. She was amazed at how this woman still appeared to have energy. She hoped that the trainer's long day performing at full throttle wouldn't impact how she facilitated Cybil's results.

"Hello there, sunshine!"

"Well, hello to you," Cybil said with a grin. "You still have the energy to talk through my profile?"

"Absolutely! Normally, though, you're right, I wouldn't schedule an assessment facilitation this soon after an all-day class. However, in this case, I think there will be some tremendous value in simply adding to today's information while it's still fresh for you. Did you find some good insights today? Actually, you know what? Let me grab a quick nature break and *then* let's answer that question."

"You got it! I'll be here with bells on whenever you're ready," Cybil responded and couldn't help but laugh. She hadn't said "with bells on" since she was a teenager, yet somehow the energy and charisma of this trainer had been contagious. Her enthusiasm seemed to rub off on those she encountered, and Cybil realized it was fun to just let go a bit. She had never given her Entertainer side permission to come out like this, and she wasn't really sure whether this qualified. The reaction just sort of popped out.

When the trainer returned, they sat at the small table in Cybil's office, with the door closed just in case others were still around. The trainer shared the five-page report from the comprehensive online CORE Profile with her and then clearly explained the one-page summary printout of the same report. She also gave Cybil her first homework assignment. She was to read, at her leisure, the five-page report that would confirm much of what they discussed. She'd never imagined the words "at your leisure" would apply to her, but after hearing what she'd heard earlier in the day, she had the feeling that some other things were about to change.

The trainer reviewed the first of three graphs on the summary report and asked for Cybil's agreement (see Figure 6.1). The graph showed that Cybil's answers

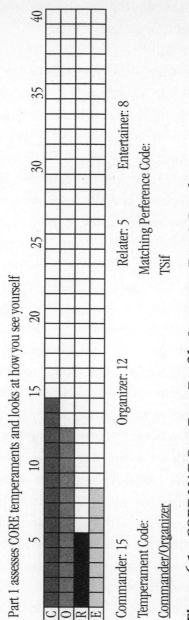

Part 1 assesses CORE temperaments and looks at how you see yourself

Commander: 15   Organizer: 12   Relater: 5   Entertainer: 8

Temperament Code: Matching Perference Code:

Commander/Organizer   TSif

Figure 6.1 CORE MAP One Page Profile Summary Part 1 Graph

Source: CORE® Profile.

indicated she was a strongly dominant Commander with a secondarily dominant Organizer trait set.

This graph revealed how Cybil saw herself based on her answers to the questions. The results were accurate, with the bar signifying "Commander" longer than any of the others. Her "Organizer" trait was second, and "Relater" had the shortest bar of all. No wonder she struggled at times with understanding the needs of others. She was task-focused and driven to get things done properly, but not so good at empathy (unless it came to her son or someone who didn't seem to understand that "moving on" and "getting stuff done" was the "right" way to be).

The bars on the second graph represented how Cybil currently functions (see Figure 6.2).

The graph was broken down into the functions Cybil was familiar with from the Myers-Briggs profile, and it even used the same language, which the trainer explained were from the works of Hippocrates and Carl Jung. It was not new information that our brains operate on basic functions, and there were a plethora of profiles that divvy up the information differently, some accurately and some not. The labels in the second graph were introverted versus extroverted, sensing versus intuitive, and feeling versus thinking.

Cybil wasn't sure how the results could be so different from the first graph. The second graph indicated that she was first a Commander and then an Entertainer. The trainer said differences between how people see themselves and how they function, what the Part 1 and 2 graphs represent respectively, are quite normal. Yet, when Cybil read the descriptions of Commander/Entertainer and

Part 2 assesses your preferences (how you relate, see the world, and process information).

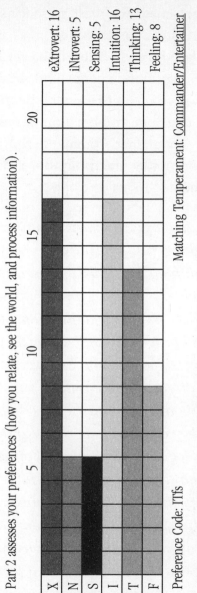

	eXtrovert: 16
	iNtrovert: 5
	Sensing: 5
	Intuition: 16
	Thinking: 13
	Feeling: 8

Preference Code: ITfs

Matching Temperament: <u>Commander/Entertainer</u>

Figure 6.2 CORE MAP One Page Profile Summary Part 2 Graph

Source: CORE® Profile.

123

Commander/Organizer in the online evaluation book, it actually made more sense. She wasn't especially comfortable claiming an Entertainer label, even as the second most dominant label, but when the trainer asked which combination gave her more energy and would be her choice if she had to live on an island with people who did nothing but treat her as one combination or the other, she chose Commander/Entertainer. Commander/Organizer just sounded boring and not as much fun, but it did describe the way she felt she had to act at work.

The Commander/Organizer was described as an extroverted, thinking, and sensing type. They function primarily in thinking mode, with the sensing mode coming in second. This inclines their thinking toward objects and facts. Extroverted thinking types are very logical and pragmatic in the way they see the world. The actions of people with extroverted thinking are almost entirely dependent upon intellectual conclusions. Although they may feel as deeply as the feeling types, they base their decisions and actions on intellect and logic rather than on their emotional responses. With sensing as their secondary trait, Commander/Organizers are critical thinkers who see both the big picture and the details that create it. The extroverted attitude inclines behaviors toward active, as opposed to passive, and energy is gained from activity and/or interacting with others. Commander/Organizers are most effective and most content in the midst of

serious, businesslike activities, and they prefer orderly,
efficient environments where they can self-manage.[1]

This described exactly how Cybil conducted herself at work, and when the trainer asked her to rate how well this description fit her on a scale of 1 to 10, with 10 being spot-on in its accuracy, she gave it a 7. It sounded stoic to her, but it was also what allowed her to not show emotion at work.

The description of the Commander/Entertainer preference that showed up in Cybil's evaluation of how she actually functioned

indicated that she was an extroverted, thinking, and intuitive type. Because these types function primarily in intuitive mode, they are very expansive in the way they approach the world and are highly oriented to future possibilities. When looking at facts and external events, they tend to look beyond rather than at them. They look at the motives behind the behaviors of people and intuit outcomes. They display an external attitude of expectancy that gives them a look of confidence or, in extreme cases, arrogance. With thinking as their secondary function, Commander/Entertainers tend to base their decisions and actions on intellect and logic rather than on their emotional responses, although their expansive approach to life may cause them to appear quite emotional at times. The extroverted attitude

---

[1] Excerpt from the CORE MAP Online Evaluation book. Copyright © 2012 COREMAP.com. All Rights Reserved.

inclines behaviors toward active as opposed to passive,
and their energy is gained from activity. As double
extroverts, Commander/Entertainers function best where
there is plenty of activity and lots of people contact.[2]

Cybil read that description and rated it as a 10, wondering whether someone had already written her biography. The description sounded just like her and reflected exactly how she had grown up behaving, even to the point of showing arrogance in the extreme cases where she was overconfident about what she was doing and where she was going.

The trainer responded to Cybil's stunned silence by saying, "In my experience, I have seen a lot of people who say they are one way at home and one way at work. What I find is that if you have to put on the mask of someone else at work, it creates stress for the authentic you. That stress causes our negative behaviors to come out and is at the root of why many people act in a way that causes them to be labeled (or perceived) as difficult."

The trainer then asked, "Does it take a lot of energy for you to act as though Organizer is your second most highly developed, or natural, trait?"

No one had ever asked Cybil that question, and, frankly, she'd never thought of her behavior in terms of energy. She just did what she had to do at warp speed in order to accomplish her daily task list. She slowly started to nod and then became more confident as she said, "Yes.

---

[2]Excerpt from the CORE MAP Online Evaluation book. Copyright © 2012 COREMAP.com. All Rights Reserved.

Make Difficult People Disappear

Yes, it does take an exceptional amount of energy. I never thought of it that way before."

"I used to do the same thing, and as a Commander I still make my to-do lists, don't worry. But here's what I used to do. Because of the way I was raised, I perceived that Commander traits were not valuable. I convinced myself that the only way I could demonstrate appropriate behavior was to be soft, mild-mannered, and never utter a cross word. Trying to take my off-the-chart Commander personality and fit it into daily into a Relater box created a stress on my entire system. The Commander behaviors did not fit in a Relater box, and they were bursting at the seams to get out."

Cybil could relate to people acting in a way they thought they needed to for approval from others, and she knew firsthand how stressful this could be.

The trainer continued, "So, my soft demeanor came out with an edge of condescension because it wasn't natural. It was being filtered through a layer of ambition, internal drive, and impatience, and when I simply couldn't suppress it anymore, well, out it came. That caused me to be in the Commander mode only when I was mad or frustrated or angry, and thus that type of behavior, which was exactly the behavior I was trying to *suppress*, came out far more often than it normally would. It was an incredibly vicious cycle that began when I was really young and became a habit. It wasn't until I started using the CORE Profile tool that I was able to give myself permission to be who I was."

The word *permission* stood out to Cybil. There it was. Giving herself permission to be who she was. Had she really not given herself permission to be who she was?

Surely it could not be as simple as acting one way at work because she thought that was what others expected. She had allowed the company culture or some external source to dictate her internal behavior instead of giving herself permission to be herself.

It seemed odd when she thought about it intellectually (as Commander/Entertainers did). She had assumed that Entertainer traits, which were natural to her, would be labeled flighty, ditzy, unprofessional, or childish. Yet there was nothing in the paragraph she read that even hinted at such descriptions for Entertainer traits.

The trainer said, "Based on the differences I see in parts 1 and 2 of your graph, there is a bit of 'faking it until you make it' in your work life, but I also suspect that some of this exists in your personal life, based on what I see in part 3. Is that true? Is there anything going on at home that might be causing you to see yourself one way and then act another way?"

She wasn't sure whether it was the directness of the question, her own fatigue at the end of the day, the rapport she had with this woman, or all three that caused her to divulge the lightbulb that just went off in her mind and openly share what she was thinking. She had never anticipated being quite this open with a professional colleague whom she barely knew, but maybe the timing was right to just trust her instincts and open the vest where she kept all her cards. It was a risk that for reasons unknown she was willing to take.

"When I go home, I feel like I am the only one who sees the need for any order or sense of urgency. Actually, what I realized earlier today is that my husband is a Relater, which

I actually already knew but couldn't articulate using this language, and my son is an Entertainer. Again, no surprise."

Cybil continued, "I am the one who makes sure we have what we need on the grocery list in time for the next day's meals. I'm the one who makes sure the house is clean and the bills are paid on time. I'm the one who sees the need to get up early so that I can direct the day's start and manage our son before I take him to school. My husband takes a more laid-back attitude about our life and life in general, whereas my son thinks life is one big party, but then again he's only eight. No wonder I act like an Organizer at home. It's the missing piece of our family, and I'm the only one who is seeing the need to do these things."

"Are you the only one with the *ability* to see the need, or are you the one who sees the need *fastest*? Remember, Commander/Entertainers have an inherent need to get things done. They thrive when they are surrounded by activities that they can get done and feel accomplished about. Heck, cleaning toilets used to show up on my to-do list . . . still does sometimes."

They both had a good giggle at that one. Cybil found the question posed by the trainer to be perceptive. She already knew the answer, but she felt like it was bigger than that.

"I don't think I'm the *only* adult in the family with the ability, but perhaps the only one who will take that initiative over just letting it go and having fun. I have a hard time letting things go and being laid back. Though I will say that somehow my husband did manage to take care of himself and get these things done before we were married. Clearly, he just did it differently than I would."

She finished her sentence with a look of surprise on her face as she realized the value of her sentence. It wasn't that he didn't do things or couldn't get things done, it was that he did them *differently* than she did. There was the crux of the issue.

"I'm not sure you have as hard a time letting things go as you do with letting yourself go and having a little fun. It's funny, actually. I see so much of myself in you, and odd as that might be to say, it's also one of the reasons we clicked immediately. People with similar personality preferences connect very quickly on levels that are often not conscious. We certainly did connect at that luncheon, as if we'd known each other for years."

That was certainly true. The trainer seemed like the only one at the table who was interesting to talk with. All they did during the luncheon was banter about the speaker's quirks or one woman's choice of "professional" attire that they both thought was better suited for a Halloween party with an "Elvira Meets the Girl Scouts" theme. They had laughed out loud much of the time and scheduled a meeting to talk business nearly immediately after the luncheon. Cybil felt like she'd known this trainer for much longer than a few weeks.

The trainer then asked her a powerful question.

"When was the first time you got the message that it wasn't okay to be emotional or fun-loving or to relax?"

Cybil shared what came to mind. "Fun was usually a planned event when I grew up. There were birthday parties with exquisitely decorated cakes, and fun ended punctually on holidays in order for my dad to get back to work or my mom to head to school. When I shared excessive emotion, I was accused of being too sensitive or whiny. I didn't really have numerous occasions to be overly happy after my parents divorced. As the only child for a number of years, I didn't have an opportunity to be the center of attention when the greater priority in a single-parent household was to put food on the table and make ends meet. My sister, Simone, who was born shortly after my father remarried, became center stage the moment she arrived and was the perfect baby and I had to fight for attention or accept that I wasn't getting it, and I guess I chose the latter."

Cybil paused and continued, "I'm not sure if I got this message from someone else, but I long ago I also decided that sharing those kinds of emotions wasn't safe or productive or really worth spending much time on. Why, is that a bad thing?"

"Oh, I'm not saying anything is bad or wrong, Cybil. It's all a matter of whether it works for you, and it sounds like when you were growing up, keeping those emotions to yourself, for a variety of reasons, worked for you. I'm just not so sure it does now. Are you?"

"I'd like to be more fun-loving, but I'm afraid nothing would ever get done. It just feels like this is how I should be."

"And that, my friend, is a trap many of us get stuck in. The real question might be, 'Is this how you *want* to be, or is this how you think you *should* be?'"

Cybil realized her answer was no.

She felt as if she was hearing another clue to becoming comfortable with being herself. She wanted to be more fun. She wanted to be less rigid. For most of her life, she'd wanted to be seen as someone who was fun to be around, but she'd never been able to quite get there.

"Well, this may help to explain some things before I answer that question. I've been thinking about my parents, and as much as I'd like to say I've outgrown their influence, maybe I haven't. Does that always stick with us? Does it always go back to the story of our childhood?"

The trainer smiled in a noncommittal sense, but also seemed to nod. Cybil continued, "If I were to imagine my father's one-page summary sheet and his graphs, it occurs to me that he would see himself as a Commander, but as I see him now, he seems to function so much more as a Relater. Do we change as we get older?"

"That's a great question! In fact, we might change, but it's not because we are changing who we are or what is most natural to us, but more that we are going home. Think about men whose goal it is to ride off into the sunset and be by themselves."

Cybil responded, "He hasn't gotten an earring or a Harley, but my father has become more solitary, more laid-back, and less angry over time. He was very, very angry when I was growing up, and I always thought that I was doing something wrong."

"Well that makes sense. If you have to live your life as a Commander when you're actually a Relater, it could cause some internal conflict and a great deal of stress. Men are often expected to be the head of household, and if your father had to let go of being laid-back and instead had to take charge or run a business or deal with any kind of crisis causing repeated and rapid decision making, then this would have stressed out his normally laid-back Relater behaviors. He would have been quite volatile as a Relater under that much stress and perhaps even truly conflicted at the loyalty he wanted to share with his new family in spite of your parents' divorce."

Cybil took in the information. There were clues coming in from all angles, and it was starting to explain so much.

The trainer then asked, "Did he become fiercely loyal to his new family, including your sister? And didn't you also describe your husband as a Relater? Interesting how that happened, huh? Maybe you are 'going home' in a variety of ways."

Cybil knew exactly what she meant, and several things started to dawn on her. The interesting thing was that in order to be herself, Cybil started to realize that she didn't have to do anything differently, but rather to stop doing some things that had merely become a habit out of what she believed she needed to do to cope or survive certain situations.

Before Cybil could drift off in her own thoughts, the trainer went on, "Besides, if your father was a true Commander, then you likely wouldn't be a Commander. What usually happens, in fact in, 97 percent of the hundreds of profiles that I have personally reviewed, is that in a family of four, each member of the family demonstrates one of the quadrants as their dominant preference. What quadrant would you say your mom occupies?"

That one is easy, Cybil thought. Her mom was nearly a genius and yet oh-so linear. She was analytical, logical, and linear but also emotional, now more than before.

Cybil answered, "I would be willing to bet money on her being an Organizer/Relater."

"Well, that would make complete sense, but we also have to be careful with assuming her dominant preference without her input or data. She could have been acting out of conditioned Organizer due to other factors. But, if your guess happens to be accurate and if your father is really a Relater who acted like a Commander and thus exhibited a lot of stress-induced behaviors, and your mom is an Organizer, but has the emotional underpinnings of a Relater, then they would have had some form of communication using the Relater commonality. You would have arrived in the world, perhaps perceived that the Relater and Organizer preferences were already taken or something to that affect, and adopted Commander or Entertainer traits. Since I see your natural ability to get things done drives you, I'd say Commander is natural and Entertainer is secondary but that it was never really invited to come out or you never perceived it was safe long term to show up and stick around. Your father's negative Commander behaviors and your mom's possibly authentic Organizer task force would have created a scary combination and environment for you as a child. Does that sound reasonable?"

Not only did it seem reasonable, but it felt like things had completely fallen into place. It was like the final click on a combination safe that indicated the door could now be opened. She felt like shouting out, "I see it! I see it! It was Professor Plum in the library with the candlestick!" only in this case it was Cybil in her own head, with a new set of clues and a map!

For videos and more information that will enhance what you've learned in this chapter, go to: www.MakeDifficult PeopleDisappear.com.

Chapter 7

HOPE . . . in What Others Intend Despite What They Do

A hopeful inner voice within Cybil was becoming louder and louder. She was getting the feeling that she could take back the reins of her life and her behavior. She was in control of how she felt, how she behaved, how she reacted, and how she perceived others, no matter what external influences or events she encountered in her life and what the voices in her head seemed to say some days. Intellectually, she'd always known she was in control, but somehow the CORE tool and their conversations about the origins of her decisions and life direction were giving her a tangible grip on where she needed and wanted to go from here. It was starting to answer the "Now what?" question that often surfaced with tools like this, but for her had never been answered. It was giving her hope, a great deal of hope.

They had one more graph to review on the one-page summary, and just by looking at it, Cybil had no idea how to interpret what all the boxes meant. The trainer shared with her that the part 3 graph (see Figure 7.1) showed conceptually how a person operated on an average day with increasing amounts of stress. She said it was by far the most revealing and might lead Cybil to believe that the trainer had somehow secretly installed cameras in her office the day before. Cybil's third graph showed that she was using the Commander behavior first and then Entertainer

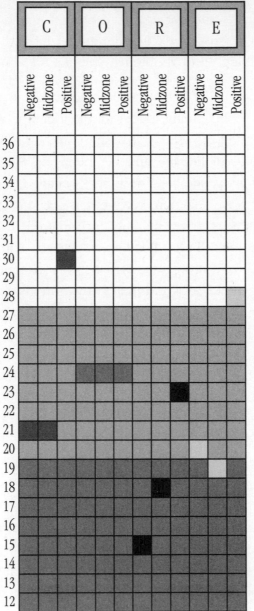

Figure 7.1 CORE MAP One Page Profile Summary Part 3 Graph

Source: CORE® Profile.

as her next course of action in an effort to mitigate or cope with the very first onset of stress. This meant that she started the day with a sense of excitement as she looked forward to accomplishing all of the items on her to-do list. At the first sign that this wouldn't be likely to happen, she reverted to humor or slight sarcasm to lighten the mood and help her cope. From then on, very little middle ground could be detected, as there were behaviors for coping with stress that she simply wasn't using and didn't realize she had available.

The analogy the trainer used to describe the part 3 graph made her behaviors and her areas of development completely clear. At no time did she say that Cybil had weaknesses, as had been the case in a previous profile in which the facilitator had literally told her she was broken. There was merely a conversation about her using those tools she thought were available to her and the suggestion that there were other tools she wasn't using because wasn't aware of them.

The trainer asked Cybil to imagine a three-drawer toolbox. Each separate drawer held different tools. The trainer compared behaviors to tools, and the three separate drawers represented Cybil's different types of behavior and would remind her that, no matter what, she had all of these preferences in her head and the ability to use any of them as she felt appropriate. She had a drawer with positive behaviors from all four preferences; a drawer with midzone, or moderately stress-induced behaviors; and a drawer with negative, or high-stress-induced behaviors. The ways in which those behaviors manifested themselves in times of stress were the order in which she accessed the three proverbial drawers in her behavior toolbox.

When she began her day, according to the graph, she opened the positive drawer and used only three of the four tools in that drawer. Not surprisingly, the Relater's positive tool was the one she hadn't seen was available to her. It didn't mean it wasn't there; it just meant it was invisible to her, perhaps stuck under the lip of her figurative drawer.

Once she had utilized all the positive tools that she thought were available, she then reached for her midzone behavior drawer in an effort to cope with or mitigate the continuing stream of stress. In this drawer, the graph showed that she didn't use the midzone Entertainer behavior to deal with the stress of her day. The fact that she didn't use this to emotionally vent or to recharge herself when faced with stress indicated that she was the last person on her list that she focused on appreciating. This was not terribly surprising, but she was now able to consciously make changes to her behavior. Here again was her cheat sheet of what to do next in order to feel she was handling issues more effectively. When someone told her to relax, it affected her as if it were a strongly profane insult. She didn't have *time* to relax and had never appreciated the insinuation that she was too uptight. The direction to *relax* reminded her that emotions were not safe to share, even mild frustration, and it sent her into a realm of irritation and anger that few other words came close to creating.

Now, she simply understood that using the midzone Entertainer tools and expressing herself more would be an effective way to avoid bottling up her emotions. When she bottled up her expressive emotions, it led to a quick release of negative behavior that came out first as a midzone, then negative, Organizer wrapped tightly around details and trying to control every scintilla of input and then as an aggressive Commander impatient and irritated by how much the analysis had slowed the pace of productivity.

It all boiled down to being confident enough to be who we really were, but also have a clear picture of who exactly that was and what we did when we didn't feel we could be authentic. At some point in the facilitation (Cybil couldn't remember when), the trainer had shared with her that part of the reason they didn't just give out the five-page report and summary without guidance from a trainer was that the creators of the CORE Profile, Dr. Sherry Buffington and Gina Morgan, had discovered in their research that an astounding 54 percent of the population didn't know themselves well enough to accurately self-report and needed a facilitator to help them find their way "home", while 38 percent were moderately self-aware and would still gain valuable insights from a tool such as this.

At least Cybil knew she wasn't the only person who held in parts of who she was, but she also knew she was the only person with the ability to change that for herself.

The assured increase in self-management after learning the profile results was part of what had convinced her that these profiles and the training class were the right thing to do for both the team and their company. Now, instead of feeling browbeaten, she felt significantly empowered to make changes, most of which consisted of no longer doing things that weren't natural to her. It was a truly exhilarating and liberating feeling, and she couldn't wait to get started, though she also knew she'd already begun.

In the end, Cybil got a bit of homework on which behaviors to bring out more often and sooner than she had previously thought appropriate. Her biggest homework assignment, though, was to give herself permission to be who she was and to have a little more fun with it. The homework would have been different if her Entertainer hadn't been so neglected. In other words, she was confident an authentic Organizer would not be asked to work on "going out and having fun." Then again, she was also now confident that she was not an authentic Organizer.

Their facilitation meeting ended with her new homework assignments and a heartfelt hug between these two women who had become friends through the course of the day, through this facilitation conversation, and in fact since the day they met. Cybil did not take for granted the immediate connection that had occurred between her and the trainer, which facilitated the immediate connection between them. This trainer now knew more about her than most of her good friends.

Cybil had a lot to think about, and they were both satisfied to call an end to the evening. Their stomachs were growling loudly. Cybil realized she still had to think about dinner for her family, and the trainer, too, began to act like a hungry baby bird, with repeated yawns. Though Cybil was physically tired, she didn't have the same drained feeling she often experienced when she poured herself into her car at the end of a workday.

It was all fascinating to her, and Cybil could think of nothing else on the way home. It was like figuring out one big puzzle, trying to make all the pieces come together, but without a picture as a guide. But the beauty of not having the puzzle-box picture was that she could now create her own scene.

This new found permission to be herself made her wonder whether the criticism she had received at certain times in her life was because she had chosen not to be herself, and the suppression had stressed out her Commander to such an extent that it almost always presented itself in the negative. That simple phrase would have made no sense to someone who didn't have the frame of reference she now had, but somehow it succinctly put together the pieces of the puzzle.

She had believed for years that her core was indeed flawed, yet that picture on her proverbial puzzle box was fading fast. She also was starting to see that finding a mate who wanted her had taken priority over finding herself. It wasn't really a husband she had been looking for as much as unconditional and consistent love and support. That need did not come from someone else but from within.

She thought about her marriage and her husband, Dave. Was the need for support the reason she had married Dave, or did she really love and respect him for who he was and because he loved her? Was he the love of her life, or the one who ensured she lived a life that included constant love, even though that love at times seemed smothering?

The trainer's description for Relater behaviors had nailed Dave's behavior, and it was uncanny how much she now understood about what he did and why. She also knew she was only scratching the surface, and it would never change the fact that his behavior was the opposite of hers.

143

Something the trainer had said earlier that day about Commanders also resonated with her. It was about respect. For Cybil and for Commanders in general, respect was often more powerful or appealing than love without respect. That didn't mean love wasn't important; it just meant that without respect, a deep and trusting love was difficult, if not impossible, to maintain.

Cybil began to wonder if she actually respected Dave or just saw his difficult behavior as something that she had to continue to tolerate for the sake of her family. He had chosen to love and accept her for who she was, and he cared about her more than anyone ever had, but was it enough? Could she find a way to respect who he was and how he operated?

She had blamed others her whole life for what they did to her and how she felt, but in a way she'd never before experienced, she now felt she had the power to truly take responsibility for her own behavior and stop blaming. She was holding on to all the reasons and blame that no longer served her well and were keeping her from being the wonderful person she really was. She was being the difficult person in her life and others seemed to be showing up in response to her behavior. She was the difficult person in some other people's lives and had been seeing many of them through a set of "difficult-colored" glasses. It was truly starting to make some sense in her own head. She decided to play with the concept for a moment.

She asked herself out loud in her car, "Would things be different if I loved myself?"

What would happen if she didn't need to be constantly reminded that she was lovable, or if she believed in herself enough to no longer need reminding of her value? Would she be less harsh with those who were different than she was or, more important, didn't spend their time doing things that would help to make her look better and thus get more approval? Would she have made a choice to marry a man she didn't respect as much as she should but whom she needed to remind her she was loved? What did that say for his confident decision to marry her since he knew who he was?

What if she hadn't been trying her whole life to be the kind and mild-mannered person that her inner Commander couldn't even draw as a stick figure, much less embody without significant effort? How much further along would she be now? What would her life be like now? How much happier might she be? More productive? More fulfilled?

She began to wonder whether all that she had believed up until now was a lie, and she felt a little silly, but also believed that life taught us what we needed to learn. In her opinion, the path she'd been on had been purposeful, if not conscious. That alone reassured her that a momentary feeling of self-doubt was fine, but that more than a moment wasn't necessary. She'd been where she'd been so that she could get where she was supposed to go.

Dave told her how amazing she was daily. He made her feel loved and valued and cherished. He reminded her of her strength, value, and power on the many occasions she didn't care to believe it or couldn't convince herself. He put her on a pedestal. In the beginning he had spent gobs of money on her to prove it and in an attempt to break through her barrier of lack of trust in their differences and in his love. It was indeed a vicious cycle and one she was tired of living. Dave respected and cared for her, and she needed to learn to better understand him, too. She was beginning to see where the challenges had come from, how long she'd held on to them, and how to let them go and move forward.

It was amazing how much multitasking the brain could manage while she drove on two highways, three side streets, and into a drive-thru restaurant. If someone had asked Cybil how she got there, she couldn't have said, but now she had to put her life on hold to figure out what her family would have for dinner.

"May I take your order?"

The loud, static-filled, barely audible voice squalled through the microphone at Boston Market. She started to order "Another life," but shifted those thoughts around to the back of the figurative lazy Susan in her head and went with three three-piece chicken meals. Ben would eat an entire drumstick and build a building from green beans, but the leftovers would keep. Tonight she might actually help him build his green bean building, or she might even build one of her own. Wouldn't that surprise them all? She would enjoy a relaxing dinner and night without her BlackBerry being the focal point; replacing it with the hope of a new beginning and the intentional and conscious granting of permission to be the real her.

"Excuse me, may I add another order of green beans to that?"

For videos and more information that will enhance what you've learned in this chapter, go to: www.MakeDifficult PeopleDisappear.com.

Chapter 8

WHEELS . . . of Motion Not Attached to a Bus

That evening was one of the nicest that Cybil could remember them having together as a family. They relaxed, ate dinner, and talked about each other's day: Dave's current project for a big client and Ben's success at the bake sale and his new friend. In between large bites of drumstick and his green-bean-building efforts, Ben described this friend as a very serious type who kept cleaning up the sprinkles that fell off his cookies and landed on the table. She was the one who had been put in charge of collecting the money for the bake sale. The girl, who kept a running total of sales, had fussed at Ben for offering discounts to those who would buy three or more cookies.

Ben was the quintessential salesman, and his new friend was his opposite in so many ways. Cybil couldn't help but think of her as a budding Organizer preference. It wouldn't have surprised her if this young lady showed up as a CPA at Ben's class reunion one day. Cybil also cautioned herself to remember that people have all kinds of experiences that could cause them to hide who they are and act like someone else. She hoped this wouldn't happen to this little girl, whom she had never met, and taught Ben how to compliment her (or at least an Organizer dominant preference) by mentioning very specific actions when he told her she did a great job managing the bake sale money and pricing. Cybil then amazed Ben with a green-bean-building masterpiece of her own. They all laughed and joked about it as they did the dishes.

Dave especially noticed what seemed to be a mellower Cybil. He commented on it as they got ready for bed. He then simply held her tight and told her he loved her as they drifted off to sleep. Something told him she was in deep thought or transition and was just in need of a little TLC. As she lay next to her husband, she realized that no matter the lack of respect, their differences, and even their difficulties, one thing she felt was clear: She was loved and maybe there were times when that was more important. This time it helped her relax and fall immediately to sleep.

The routine was the same as always the next morning, but this time Cybil laughed at her usual fervor. Her to-do list and desire to have a waterproof notepad in the shower seemed less urgent. She didn't even bother to check her BlackBerry until after she had her coffee, resting assured that whatever was "on fire" here or with her overseas client would get done as it always had. Instead, she spent five extra minutes snuggled up next to the man who made her feel loved and five extra minutes letting Ben choose between three pairs of patterned pants. The trainer had shared with her the day before that Entertainers need to have freedom from control and detail and that they were the ones who most often gravitated toward bright colors, patterns, and shiny things. She was practicing giving Ben a bit more control in his choice of attire. This morning, she realized it wasn't as loud or intolerable as she once thought, and she actually enjoyed looking at all the different colors in his closet and drawers. It made her laugh to herself, as she was aware of how her perceptions of what constituted "difficult" were changing.

Fortunately, this morning there were no cookie crises and no frustrated feelings, only a relaxed contentment and a growing confidence. Cybil decided to hire a housekeeper and to let go of the stress she always felt in coming home and picking up after everyone all the time. She was determined to continue to take action on what she'd learned.

When she got to the office, she ran into her boss in the hall and gave him a smile. She asked about his son's Little League game before mentioning yesterday's missed meeting, and he seemed eager, though in a reserved manner, to share his story. He also asked Cybil what she thought of the class and whether the follow-up meeting with the trainer and the team was still a go. She smiled and said that the class was likely one of the best leadership decisions they had made in a long time and certainly would be a life-changing experience for her and she suspected many others, though she didn't go into much detail. After she confirmed the meeting with him, she left him with a "tell me more" look on his face and headed for her office.

He didn't bring up the need for the two of them to meet, so she left it alone. They could address it later that afternoon. They would be in meetings all morning, and she suspected that whatever he needed to address with her had either lost its sense of urgency or that he'd handled it. It was a new feeling for her to let go of the need to radically control everything in her world.

151

She could hear team members arriving one by one, and by 9:30 she had made the first cleanup sweep through her in-box and put out three overseas fires for other team members. Then she decided to take a walk and connect with some of the folks on her team. They worked so hard, but rarely saw her greet them in the morning or thank them for their efforts.

She wanted to connect with them, but had never felt it to be a valuable use of her time to do so and, up until yesterday, had assumed that they all knew and understood how busy she was. It was indeed enlightening to learn that others didn't think the way she did. In some ways, she wished they did, but she now knew it wasn't a character flaw or fault of theirs that they didn't. Nor was it a fault of hers to act as she did. Maybe they could all simply exercise a bit more conscious thought about their actions. They could be more conscious of what they said to each other and how they said it. In fact, this entire training course had been brought in on the premise that they were trying to ensure they had all the right team members in the right seats on the bus, to borrow a phrase from the book *Good to Great*. Cybil now thought it might be more appropriate to determine where the bus was headed, what was important to those driving it, and what they needed to keep driving in the direction of the company's goals (versus making sure they were all in the right seats).

Her conversations were revealing. She heard comments and stories from each team member, without prompting or solicitation, about how the training session had positively impacted their lives. Many were enjoying closer connections with their friends and loved ones seemingly

Make Difficult People Disappear

already. Others told stories about their commute home. One shared how he could see that the clerk at his local 7-Eleven was an Entertainer by the fact that she talked with every customer for a few minutes while simultaneously greeting those who came in. People were using the information that they had learned in the class the day before. They now had knowledge of all the tools and were using the simple power of conscious awareness and paying attention to make a significant difference in the number of people they perceived as difficult.

Maybe this information would be more than the campaign of the week kind of initiative and would have a lasting impact. Maybe she wasn't the only one who was learning how to consider giving herself permission to be who she was after the facilitation of her personal profile results. There was a palpable buzz in the office, and she was glad she had taken the time to walk around. Cybil made a note to continue this check-in process on a daily basis as part of her new routine. It felt like she had been handed a magic wand in some ways. Difficulty and difficult people hadn't shown up yet on this the first day after the training class.

■ ■ ■

Each person in the class had been scheduled for a facilitation meeting similar to the one Cybil had experienced, to discuss the results of his or her own comprehensive CORE Profile. A few had had their sessions prior to the class, and those were the ones who seemed to get a great deal more out of the overall experience, but most were scheduled for the coming days, and folks were far more excited about them now, since the trainer had explained what they were about and had shown how they could be used. Her style, much as she had promised, had broken the ice and allowed each participant to build his or her own rapport with this woman. None had known her previously, but there was a feeling that they were all in this together now and professional colleagues, if not friends.

Initially, some of the team members suspected that the information might be used in an effort to downsize or eliminate those who didn't fit the mold. Some were even afraid of being fired, but as Cybil walked around, she found even the most resistant ones were making an effort to use knowledge from the class. She couldn't wait to see what would happen after each person's individual session.

Cybil was so glad she had opted to go to lunch with the trainer the day they'd met instead of canceling, as had been her inclination. That choice would be one she would remember and treasure forever.

The meeting to debrief the training was scheduled to begin in a half hour, and as she headed back to her desk, she noticed on her cell phone screen that she had missed two calls. Both were from her sister, Simone. Rather than emitting her usual exhausted sigh, Cybil thought fondly of Simone and her softer side.

She decided to call her back and check in before her meeting. "Hey, Sis, how are you? I'm sorry I missed your call. I was actually walking around talking to my team members."

"You were *what*?" It was noisy in the background. Simone sounded like she was in a convention hall surrounded by hundreds of people.

"I was walking around . . . oh, never mind. Where are you?"

"I want to hear more about you walking around. That doesn't sound like you, but you can tell me more about that later. I just called to say hello and tell you that you were right. Philip's not having an affair. He was just swamped, and when I sat down and finally talked with him about it and told him what I needed, for some reason he seemed to understand. I did what you've always said to do. I stuck to the facts, showed some emotion, but still managed to get to the point, and truthfully, I also picked a time when he wasn't as stressed or rushed—also like you've told me before."

Cybil was smiling from ear to ear in the realization that for years she had given her sister guidance on how to handle Philip. She had been coaching Simone to address him in the language he understood, to recognize what he needed, and to improve the effectiveness of her communication. She was pretty sure now that he was a Commander and realized that, unconsciously, she'd been conveying to Simone what his needs were because they were the same as her own in many cases! It was great confirmation for her, and it seemed funny to her when she thought about how things worked out. She knew more about herself than she thought, yet on a conscious level she was only now beginning realize it. It also explained why Cybil at times didn't like Philip's behavior. It embodied the very style of behavior, Cybil wasn't fond of in herself. She was quick to label his behavior, and the irony is he probably thought similarly of hers.

"That's incredible, Sis, and I'm so proud of you and also so excited for you and glad to hear the news! I bet you are relieved and excited, too!"

"Well, I am excited, but not only for that reason. We had a long talk after I brought it up, and it seemed to bond us together in a way that we hadn't bonded before. We connected on a level where we both felt heard and clearly understood. Then . . . Sis, are you sitting down?"

"Uh-oh. Yes, I am. What's going on, and where the heck are you?" The noise in the background was getting louder, and Cybil could hear what sounded like boarding calls at an airport.

"We're at the airport, Sis. We're on our way to Paris to meet his family. He wants to introduce them to his new fiancée!"

"Oh my gosh! Are you serious?"

"I am! He asked me last night, and if we hadn't gotten wrapped up in celebrating, I would have called you sooner. He proposed and then handed me two tickets. Somehow we made it all work, and it's coming together!"

"Oh, Simone, that is amazing. I want to hear the whole story. When are you coming back?"

"They are calling us to board now, so I have to go, but I promise I'll fill you in as soon as we get back. If I can, I'll send you an e-mail from Paris. I'll be back in a week. Sis, I love you and thank you."

"I'm so happy for you. Give Philip a kiss for me, and tell him I'm looking forward to being the sister he never had and celebrating in style with you both! Travel safe, and I love you, too!"

They hung up, and Cybil realized that she had shown more emotion in that one phone call while at work than she had shown her sister in some time. The response, even in her newly engaged state, was wonderful to hear, and it felt like she and her sister had connected in a way that they hadn't been able to do in quite a while.

There were going to be many occasions worth celebrating in her future, and even if not all were as large as the marriage of her sister, she felt as though she could really enjoy her life and celebrate and share her emotions.

She walked down the hall to her boss's office with the grin of a Cheshire cat and was the first to arrive at the meeting. Her boss still had a puzzled look on his face and spoke to her quickly, before the others arrived.

"Okay, what's going on with you? This morning you seem more relaxed than I've seen you in years; you mentioned a life-altering experience out of a mere training class; and now you look like the cat who swallowed the canary. What's going on?"

"All good things, I promise. I think I've merely realized some things about myself and about how I work and how I no longer wish to operate. Oh, that and my sister just told me she's engaged. She's headed to Paris to meet her fiancé's family as we speak."

"Well, that *is* good news, and give her my congratulations."

Cybil smiled and nodded in response.

"I've been wondering what happened in this class. If this is any indication of the results we'll get from the others, then I think we should have paid twice as much and done this years ago. Can you tell me more about these changes later? It might have some relevance to what I wanted to talk with you about yesterday. Oh, and did I see you walking around the office this morning talking to your teammates?"

"I think you're right about the class, and, yes, I was. I wanted to connect with them and check in to see how they are using the information from yesterday. I think it is important to make sure we are getting a good return on our investment." She said it and then immediately felt her shoulders tighten and her face become serious as she slipped into Organizer mode. Only this time, she actually felt it physically. *"So this is what it feels like,"* she thought. *"Well, this is easy. All I have to do is stop putting on that mask."*

What she said then surprised even her.

"Well, that, and I truly wanted to connect with my team. It's been too long, and they've all worked very hard. They deserve to know their boss cares about them as people."

Her boss smiled at her for the second time in two days, and he looked immensely pleased, though somewhat puzzled at her new perspective about what her team members deserved. This was all new to him, but he liked what he saw.

His intent the previous day had been to encourage her to act a bit more approachable and personable toward those she led. He had heard the labels for Cybil being tossed around, and he suspected her manner was inhibiting productivity on the team. He wasn't sure, but something told him the problem he had been ready to address might no longer exist. He would keep an eye out, but was glad to see this side of Cybil and hoped it would continue.

■ ■ ■

The trainer lit up the room with her confidence and charisma. She truly possessed a contagious sense of both and it was hard not to be enthused about or at least interested in whatever was about to be addressed in a meeting with her.

"How are you this morning? And how is the team? Are you seeing some results already?"

They relayed some of the morning conversation and also shared the progress they were making in communicating with their coworkers and families. They chatted socially for a moment and then quickly got down to business.

The trainer shared a significantly complicated spreadsheet with examples of profiles and benchmarks of employees and teams. She explained how it would all be filled in after each person had completed their facilitation. She shared that, much as other tools on the market helped an organization to balance out strengths and areas of development, the CORE Profile tool would also provide this type of information, but would include the "now what" steps that were often missing with other programs. It clearly aided in making decisions about how to form teams, fill vacancies, seek out certain criteria in hiring, make moves among talented team members to strengthen multiple groups, and how to design training classes around the skill gaps that were missing.

The trainer said, "Once everyone has the knowledge and the raised awareness about how to self-manage their own behavioral choices, you'll find a dramatic reduction in instances of conflict. People will no longer readily take the behavior of others so personally. Now, mind you, that doesn't mean there will never be any disagreements, but it does mean they won't last as long or cause as much long-term damage or as many breakdowns in productivity and teamwork. Plus you'll also be able to use this with your succession planning and filling gaps as they occur with natural attrition or expansion. You won't just be filling gaps, but will have guidance and a plan on what types of characteristics and preferences are best suited to that role or position and be able to make informed decisions about internal and external candidates, promotions, and lateral moves. With this type of knowledge and a solidly reinforced culture of people who all know about this information and are encouraged to use it, you will truly experience an employee base that stays longer, complains less, and produces more."

Cybil's eyebrow rose, accompanied by a soft but hesitant smile, and she continued to take notes.

"How we use this information at this point will make a world of difference. Here is the multiphase approach I recommend: We are now in phase 1. They have had an introductory class and are in the process of completing their own profiles among the leadership team. Phase 2 includes populating the spreadsheet with the dominant and secondary preference types for each person. I'll then go over that with you to determine whether there are any gaps between your employment needs and the existing positions. However, also in phase 2, we will want to create job descriptions or enhance the ones you already have by including the key character traits, ideal preference combination and behavior-based criteria. This is different than competencies. Now you will have job descriptions that include key behavioral traits that lend themselves to success in that role."

Cybil nodded and continued taking notes.

"In addition, one of the ways to promote achievement in the teams you lead is to benchmark your top performers in each job and determine which parts of their personality type are contributing to their success. It may be skills or experience or personality traits or both, but finding out and narrowing down the cause of their success allows you to then duplicate it and make that success scalable across your entire organization. Once we have those benchmarks for the ideal performer in each position, we can compare profiles of others in those positions and see if we need to make some major moves or have missed key criteria that lead to high performance. Does that make sense?"

The trainer seemed to pause as much to take a breath as to check in with Cybil and her boss to confirm understanding.

The boss responded, "Yes, it makes sense. And it is exactly what I think we've been wanting to do: systematically evaluate performance and development paths, but also consider that these are people we might be moving around and talking about. The other systems I've seen strike me as a bit cold or less than considerate of the fact that these are people we're talking about not just hash marks on a line item or an account on the P and L. I usually take a great deal of time to think through implementation decisions like this one, and though I'm quite certain this is not something you or your company does for free, I've got to tell you, if the results I've seen thus far are any indication of the immediate results this information can create, I think I'm nearly convinced and quite comfortable saying we want to move forward with this."

Her boss still seemed to be wavering as he hadn't said let's begin this tomorrow or something that conveyed a sense of urgency, but it was part of his natural set of skills and preferences to not make a decision without thinking about it and ensuring it was the right one. What he had said was significant if he did, in fact, lead with dominant Organizer traits. Cybil was proud of her newfound recognition of what was happening right before her very eyes. When she realized that she would have previously been frustrated by his lack of certainty and urgency, she had to laugh at herself at the clear reminder that Organizers were never 100 percent sure on a decision until they knew without a shadow of a doubt that it was the right thing to do. She wasn't sure what had convinced him, but she could not recall her boss moving so quickly in the past to make a decision. Clearly, he was seeing results that gave him the assurance he needed. Then again, there were several things she hadn't seen in their tenure together. She wondered what else she would learn now that she was paying attention to something other than difficulty.

The trainer continued, "Excellent. I was hoping it was as clear coming out of my mouth as it was in my head. That doesn't always happen, but I'm on a roll this morning. This is the kind of project that I love to work with because you do see significant changes so quickly. It challenges me to keep the needs of each person in mind while we're achieving these results." The trainer said this with a calm authority and Cybil recognized the Commander needs from their facilitation conversation the night before: challenge, action, and results.

The trainer continued describing the phases needed to achieve their desired results. "Phase 3 would include a series of curriculums that specifically address your skill gaps. What we'll learn when they each complete the profile, much as you may remember, Cybil, is which behaviors are being used and which ones are not seen and therefore not used. With this information we can then create coursework, title it whatever you wish, and include in the course training for the very specific skills that are missing. Plus, when we have this level of data, we'll be able to balance out the classes with each personality preference and ensure maximum engagement and energy from the group so that all participants benefit and are able to gain the most and retain it far longer. And then there's the best part. I want to speak directly to your ROI concerns. Cybil, you and I briefly discussed this when we spoke after our luncheon, but I want to really paint this picture. Once we design classes for, let's say, the top five skill-based needs, and deliver those classes in the next three to six months, we will then re-administer only part 3 of the profile and provide a literal graph that shows behavior change and allows you to measure the results of your investment on the entire team, as well as each individual team member."

The trainer was almost giddy with excitement, but in a professional manner. It was clear, however, how excited she was about her subject, and Cybil couldn't help but admire this woman, who was truly passionate about her career, her chosen field, and the skill she had developed for it. She was a natural trainer, but a Commander who also need to ensure she created results that could be proven and enjoyed projects that provided a challenge. And then Cybil remembered: The trainer hadn't given herself permission to be a Commander/Entertainer until she was older—in fact, right about the time (or shortly before) she had become a professional trainer.

Cybil wondered how many people on her team were suffering from being stuck in a role that didn't allow them to use their natural gifts, skills, and talents. Cybil was looking at the results of that kind of match, and she couldn't wait to provide that for those she led.

Communicating effectively as a leader isn't about the seats on the bus (or the wheels on the bus, for that matter), it is about putting the wheels in motion to help those she had the privilege of leading to be themselves and lead themselves. From there, they could lead the customers they served with the same kind of dedication, energy, and passion as the trainer. They could all do it in the way that worked for them, but what was now clear was that they had to do it; for themselves, for the team, for the company, and for their customers. Making difficult people disappear was about to open up a world that included customers, vendors, affiliates, partners, principles, and shareholders, and Cybil could tell that her boss was nearly salivating and the positive impact he could now see this would have on the bottom line.

He asked, "Can you begin to implement the next phase immediately and keep us on track for the accelerated results program? I'd love to be able to share those quantifiable results with our board of directors at our next meeting, when we discuss human capital."

The trainer said yes, but they could see she was somewhat deflated. She paused and then went on to explain.

"*Human capital* is one of those phrases that human resources feels the need to use to explain the costs, liabilities, and expense of people who run a business. It's actually well documented and explained in a book called *Contagious Leadership*, which I would highly recommend you look into if you're interested. It describes leadership by focusing on people and changing what you call them, whether "human capital" or another term, and Chapter 1 is about how you treat them. The reality is that these are *people*, much as you shared earlier and not mere occupants of seats on some proverbial bus and not merely line items on a spreadsheet. They are the lifeblood of your company. They are the ones with whom your customers make relationships, whom they see and talk to regularly, and with whom they connect. They are also, at least most of the frontline, in need of a focus on who they are as people. In fact, most of your frontline employees have a higher development and demonstration of Entertainer and Relater traits, and this is what makes them great in sales and great with people. However, when the company leaders treat them or talk about them as if they are mere tasks to be dealt with or objects to be described to the board, then you lose some of the people-focus."

Cybil wasn't at all sure how her boss would react to this near reprimand of his use of the term *human capital.* And truthfully, it wasn't a reprimand, as the trainer's tone was kind and her passion evident, and what she said made complete and utter sense. It was all in direct alignment with everything they had learned the day before and frankly with what her boss had said earlier in the conversation, or so she thought.

The trainer continued, "In order for us to successfully transition your culture from one in which everyone sees difficult people, so to speak, to one in which we're literally working together and creating customers for life, not to mention revenue, the first place that needs to be felt and understood is at the top level of leadership, or in this case, with the board."

Without missing a beat, the words out of her boss's mouth no longer surprised her, but reminded her that things were about to change . . . for the better.

"I think you're absolutely right. I have always valued people more than we've been able to show around here and I think you just uncovered a bit of unconscious conflict between how I feel and the language I've been using. Very interesting and thank you."

He looked right at Cybil as he said it, and she got the impression he was also talking about her and her new, more personable behavior.

He went on to say, "I am also not at all sure that I could articulate to our board of directors what you've just said so well and so clearly. Perhaps you'd be able to present this information to them as well? In fact, perhaps you could explain the transformative nature of our culture, where we're headed, and the information about human cap . . . er, I mean, *those we have the privilege of leading.*"

"I would be happy to, and I think it will go a long way toward putting the wheels in motion to get where you want to go and also in keeping things rolling forward in the name of progress and higher productivity."

The meeting couldn't have been more productive; in less than an hour, they had been able to continue the momentum of the previous day's training and form a plan for future development. Cybil was excited about the changes that would take place over the next six months. She liked thinking about those she led as *people* instead of as employees for whose performance she alone was responsible. She previously had thought of the right people in the right seats on the bus as a task to check off her list. There were still certainly tasks to complete, but the bus that they were all supposed to be on, as if this were merely a ride to school and not real life, now seemed to now be taking on a more substantive form outside of the original analogy. We don't just all ride a bus and jump off at our respective classes. This is the real world, populated

167

WHEELS . . . of Motion Not Attached to a Bus

by real people, and the more we dehumanize them and the more we stress them, the more difficult they are to deal with. When that happens, the cycle seems to continue. Cybil was now certain there was a new cycle in motion for all of them and she was excited to see what lay ahead now that the bus was headed down this road.

For videos and more information that will enhance what you've learned in this chapter, go to: www.MakeDifficult PeopleDisappear.com.

Chapter 9

HABITS . . . That Help You Be You and Let Them Be Them

Over the coming weeks, Cybil and the trainer worked closely together to continue the development of her new habits. Cybil hired her as a coach, to keep up the momentum of not only an invaluable relationship, but the wealth of information that had become an indispensable resource in Cybil's life.

She'd picked up *Contagious Leadership* and a few other resources, and found renewed interest in Napoleon Hill's *Think and Grow Rich*. The books seemed to speak directly to her and allow her to maintain her focus on thoughts that were helpful, healthy, and people-oriented. Keeping her energy positive and focused helped her accomplish even more and feel more successful. The old habits were hard to break, but she now acknowledged that when her Organizer preference came out in stressful situations, she could accept it and then let it pass. She no longer continued to suppress her emotions.

Cybil was amazed at how much energy she had spent faking it for so long. Things began to improve more and more the less she faked being someone she wasn't. The trainer described it in one of their Phase 3 ongoing training sessions as "putting on the game face."

"Have any of you ever put on a game face to go to work?" she said to the class. There were a few nods and a few confused looks.

"Okay, what I mean is, have any of you ever psyched yourself up to go to work? You know what I mean. You get up and grumble, 'Oh, I'm going to work,' followed by, 'Okay, I'm going to work,' and then say with more pep, 'Okay, I'm going to work!'" (at which point she assumed a completely fake smile and stood in a cheerleader-ready position).

Through her exaggerated smile, she said, "So, if you feel the need to plaster on a fake smile at the beginning of the day, what happens to your face at five o'clock when you leave the office?"

Her face contorted to a much more distressed look, as if she had just lost control of the muscles used to smile. The rapid transition from one face to the next while she was talking made it funny to watch. But what she said next set aside the humor and made a point that stuck.

"Where are you normally going when you leave the office? Most of you are going home, right? If this is the face that you're taking with you when you go there, I want to share a little news bulletin with you. Home is not where you go when you're tired of being nice to people."

She paused. The room took it in and then laughed heartily. There was a lot more laughter in the office these days and ironically their revenue was also rising.

The courses were working, the facilitations had gone off without a hitch, and the energy level seemed charged with interest, passion, and a renewed excitement for the jobs each team member performed. They had made only a few moves based on the spreadsheet created after the facilitations, and no one had lost their position, as many had feared.

There had been some natural attrition, and, ironically, those who had been the most difficult to deal with in the first place were the ones who left. They seemed unable to handle the positive energy and focusing on people for who they were, which allowed employees to just be themselves while being productive. For their own reasons, they chose to depart from the company, and it was another affirmation that this information did indeed help to make difficult people disappear.

There were times when Cybil was still tired, but it was a resilient tired that allowed her to bounce back with simple steps or a bit of rest without needing to spend an evening as a couch potato nearing a burned-out state. She experienced this when she flew to Paris for Simone and Philip's engagement party a few weeks after their announcement; she was exhausted when she arrived, but knew enough about her own authentic needs to share her fatigue rather than faking it. She acknowledged it, took a quick nap, and then found some activities to keep herself busy—and a project that allowed her to feel in control. In no time, her energy returned, and she encountered very few stress-related feelings or behaviors as a result.

Cybil found that when she was the most tired, her old habits were much more powerful and she was more likely to revert back to her old ways, and Cybil worried about this on her Paris trip.

But she kept her cool when things became disorganized and Simone didn't speak up for something that was especially important to her. Instead of blasting her for it and encouraging her to be someone she wasn't, Cybil merely handled her sister's request behind the scenes and without incident. Her sister thanked her later, knowing Cybil had stepped in to help when she herself had been loath to make a direct conflict out of the situation. It reminded Cybil to be herself, but also to respect the needs of others while taking care of herself, appreciating her own Entertainer style and needs, and getting adequate rest.

Cybil saw the same changes in her coworkers that she saw in her relationship with her family. The team she led all reacted positively to their profile facilitations. They were using the highlights from the evaluation book to strategically plan team meetings, coaching conversations, guidelines for conflict resolution, team formation, project management, and project progress. It was truly an astounding sight to watch formerly quiet and undervalued team members take on leadership roles in a way that utilized their strengths. Cybil couldn't remember the last time someone had come to her office to complain about a team member. She was still very much involved in the team's progress, but now it had become the norm for her team members to self-manage and to manage each other's communication to come up with solutions before they came to her to merely let her know how it had been resolved.

Her relationship with Dave had reached a level that she had not anticipated after she had him complete his own CORE Profile outside of work. Their difficulties seemed

Make Difficult People Disappear

to disappear, as they now had that very cheat sheet Cybil wanted. In fact, the new tools even helped Jason, her friend and the CFO from work, create his relationship diagram report and publish it in a major magazine. The entire company had a chance to review it and contribute, but because of their familiarity with *The Five Love Languages,* Cybil and Dave had been able to add an extra dimension, and it brought them closer as they completed the project together. Dave felt needed, and Cybil found a challenge that allowed her to produce results and see action being taken on the information that changed her life and her marriage.

Ben would be nine soon, and Cybil was using all of her Entertainer traits to plan the best birthday ever. There would be no regulated end time or seat assignments, and she used her Organizer side only to keep track of his requests and to bring it all to life without blowing their budget. Outside of that, she let herself enjoy planning his party and couldn't wait to don a child-size party hat herself.

The only piece she hadn't decided upon was how she and Dave were going to give Ben his biggest birthday present. She was pretty sure he'd like it, but didn't want to risk sharing the news in front of his guests, just in case. Midway through his ninth year, Ben was going to have a little sister in his life. Their family of four would be complete, and Cybil was now fascinated by the possibility that this child might be a little Organizer, and no matter what, she and Dave were determined to let her be herself.

Life had taken on a much more relaxed feel, yet everything still somehow managed to get done, and there was certainly more to do with a new baby on the way. It was a new time and a new feeling of energy. Cybil looked forward to her future instead of dreading what might land on her desk next.

Cybil finally let go of blaming her parents, her former bosses, and even the woman who had told her she was broken. She even had a creative way of looking at the blame she released: She told the trainer one day that she had decided to no longer "lease space in my brain to all these people," thus allowing their influence to spread to all corners of her mind and guide her behavior. Before that, she had let them not only lease the space, but also move in all their own issues and make her life rather difficult. This way of viewing the personal pain from her past then showed up as the filter through which she saw so many other difficult people. She no longer saw difficult people nearly as often, and she was pretty sure they hadn't all just left the planet. The change had started with her and the way she looked at others.

Cybil's open communication and drastic progress wasn't without its periodic adventures and challenges. Tim still offered to lend a hand at every turn and claimed he did not have enough time to do his normal job in addition to all his newly created projects. Now Cybil just asked him what he thought the "right" priority was, and that usually worked to keep him on track and on task. He also thought had found a way to improve his follow through once he learned what his triggers and stressors were from his own profile results.

The team was performing at its best, and because they were doing so well, they were rewarded with more work!

At times, it felt like moving mountains to get it all done. However, Cybil now handled it differently. Instead of exhibiting frustration and desperation and using an anxiety-ridden tone that came with a runaway fear of things not getting done on her time, she would just call for a break and give the team some downtime and something else to focus on that also provided a bit of humor. It allowed her Entertainer to shine and kept her sane, but also kept the team excited about knowing she had their back and understood their needs. One time she rented a bounce house. Another time she brought in cupcakes from April's bakery decorated with caricatures of each person. April's had done a great job of putting little icing faces on each cupcake based on gender and hair color and length. It had been quite the project, but worth every moment to see the smiles and jokes about what each person looked like on the cupcakes. Even the Organizers got a good giggle.

The trainer and Cybil maintained a close friendship, and the trainer was involved throughout the long-term growth of Cybil and her team. Not only had the difficult people disappeared into thin air, but those who were more fun to be around and added to her feelings of productivity and fulfillment seemed to materialize out of that same thin air.

■ ■ ■

The trainer was not only immeasurably pleased with the progress made by Cybil and her team, but also honored to have been a part of such an initiative. She'd had her own personal struggles of trying to be one preference while

HABITS . . . That Help You Be You and Let Them Be Them

authentically being another, and she knew that sharing her learned knowledge would prove valuable to others. Reflecting on that old phrase, "Those who can, *do*; those who can't, *teach*," she now recognized that until you dealt with the conflict of inauthenticity and becoming one of those difficult people, you couldn't maintain any credibility in teaching others how to modify their own difficult behaviors. She shared so many traits with Cybil and had found it easy to guide her through rapid development, but she also knew everyone had their own story and experiences, even if they showed up in similar ways.

Today was a new day and would bring a new opportunity to experience the very techniques she taught. Today would add to her own story and maybe even give her another story to use in classes as a teaching method to help others. She had come up with the toolbox analogy when she had had her car in the shop one time and created the "Home is not where you go . . ." statement while in a conversation with a woman in the grocery store. It seemed all she had to do was pay attention to life and listen to the events around her and the relevant examples or stories she needed to convey valuable information to participants would appear, as if by magic. In fact, it seemed that much of life and work was that way.

The more we push for action or results, the more resistance shows up. The more we try to push difficult people out of our way, so to speak, the more they push back. The more we force things, the more firmly rooted they become. This was why she had become so involved in helping people discover who they were and how to work better with

Make Difficult People Disappear

others. She was able to teach them to stop pushing others into being something they weren't and to stop pushing themselves so unnecessarily as well. It was all a part of the same conversation. Stop pushing Jack Russells to be German shepherds, Entertainers to be calm and quiet, Commanders to be soft spoken, and so on. In fact, in the next class she presented a topic similar to Cybil's first training program, she had the entire room raise their hands and find a partner. She instructed them to touch hands, palm to palm, and to start gently pushing. Without any further provocation, each pair of participants reported that when the other person pushed, they pushed back. It a wonderful way to show what people do naturally and to convey the value of *allowing* instead of always pushing. And, much as she always did, the trainer took her own lesson to heart and stopped pushing things in her own world quite as much.

For this and many other reasons, she loved training-class days. It always gave her a chance to not only share knowledge and skills with others, but also to apply those very same lessons to her own life. As her clients grew, so did she. The same was true of those she worked with. As the leaders grew, so did those they led. It drove her to continue building her practice, and she worked on ways to articulate that growth leaders needed even more, *beyond* "practicing what you preach." The concept seemed much larger than that.

A new concept in progress always excited her and ignited her passion, but this was different than that usual excitement and adrenaline. She thought for a moment about Cybil's progress and the expansion of "practice what you preach" and "leadership change starts at the top" and "everything we do, say, and think believe, and how we behave is contagious" and wondered if there was much, much more to it than that. Was this really more than the random thoughts she had at times and the philosophizing she engaged in? Was she really on to something for her next training class?

This may well be the beginning of the next training class she and others needed the most. It would go beyond the basics of tested leadership theories and adages. It would enhance the ability to "know thyself, manage thyself, and cease seeing difficult people everywhere" and would propel leaders to a point where difficulty was no longer a fervent conversation but a "remember when" reference. Not only could she help others "go home," but also help them get where they wanted to go with ease, clear direction, and success. She considered calling the concept "Moving Mountains" and then set it aside on her desk to focus on and prepare for her next class.

The next day she bounced out of bed, got ready for the day, and headed out for her class with freshly printed handouts and all of her materials. This was a class she knew well, a roomful of corporate middle managers who were struggling with motivation, conflict, teamwork, communication with each other, and what she suspected was also a problem with confidence to be who they were in the face of a company culture that seemed to say, "We only value a certain type of person, and if that's not who you are, then you'd better fake it to get promoted or act as if for as long as you work here." It was familiar territory, and it excited her to think about the possibility for life-changing epiphanies that would occur over the next few months, after these managers completed her course and participated in their own CORE Profiles. She decided that the opening-class focus would be on self-esteem and confidence, as a form of internal motivation, and how both were highly contagious and part of the problem when the complaint was about a multitude of difficult people. People in general were not difficult, they were *different*, but when you coupled low confidence to be oneself with a perceived unsafe environment in which to do so and coupled a lack of understanding about different communication styles with a lack of perceived motivation to change, you created an environment in which dealing with difficult people seemed to be required skills. The truth was, sharing those skills was merely a Band-Aid for a much larger problem.

The culture didn't support or value the very people who did the work inside the company, and the effect bled out to the customers, the community, and potential employees, not to mention the people in the personal lives of those employees (those they saw when they left the office). They not only were unable to make the difficult people disappear, but also seemed to be developing them in-house by the dozens.

She arrived ahead of schedule, set up early, and then greeted each team member as they arrived for class. Her usual rapport-building skills and ability to remember the names of each participant were going to come in handy today, as this group had some challenges. Instead of dancing around the issue, she thought she would attack it directly and show her approachability earlier than she did in most programs. They needed to know she understood their perspective.

As she started her opening remarks, she could almost feel their need for permission to be real themselves. She introduced herself and defined *contagious behavior*, as she often did, using the example of how a woman might arrive at the office having ridden her broom to work and how that behavior rubs off on everyone else and is, in fact, contagious. It was their second laugh of the morning, and they had been going for only about five minutes.

Then she dove right in and said, "Do you think self-esteem and confidence are a part of the problems that leaders face?" Heads nodded tentatively.

"Do you think a lack of self-esteem or confidence is contagious?" More heads nodded in agreement.

"Well let's test this theory and see how it might apply to those of you in this room. Don't worry, I'm not going to point anyone out, but I do think that if we can eliminate the confidence deficiency, we'll also eliminate the vast majority of the difficult people you work with. Oh, well, let me ask that question first. Who in here works with or has ever worked with a difficult person?"

The participants laughed and she continued, "Now, no pointing at other people—all eyes up here. My research shows that two out of three people are walking around with a sense of low self-esteem, and I firmly believe that a lack of confidence is part what makes people feel or act difficult. Would you agree?"

Make Difficult People Disappear

They seemed to buy into this concept and were following her nicely. She could tell it was going to be a great class. They were all eager to make the problem go away, particularly all those difficult people, even if some of them were right here in the room and recognized themselves.

"So, let's test this out. I want you to look to the person on your left. If you don't know which side that is, just pick somebody. Good! Now, look to the person on the right, or your other side."

"Most of you have just looked at two other people. Excellent. Now if we adhere to the ratio that two out of three people have a low sense of self-esteem and each of you have just looked at two other people, then that means only one of you is okay. Who is it?"

She quickly raised her hand to demonstrate the behavior she was looking for, and the group erupted in laughter, with about five hands raised high in the air and lots of pointing from other people. She made her point, which allowed the ones who arrived in class acting like difficult people to relax a little. She also got them to trust that she was there to help, not to call people out on what they were doing wrong. Most were just doing the best they could. She had seemingly moved a small mountain.

Then it hit her.

"There's something I want you to observe here. We live in a culture where saying you have high self-esteem is a no-no. So I'm aware that more of you have it than actually raised your hands, but I also want you to consider what that does for your ability to work together. What you can learn from this is that most people are doing the best they know how to do and dealing with internal voices and external influences. The moment you label them as difficult, you eliminate your options for better understanding. You cease to leave the door open to understand who they are and what they need versus just what they do that is different from the way you would do it. And you build a mountain of obstacles to overcome in the way of motivation."

She paused and looked around the room, "In fact, to kick off our class today, to say thank you in advance for your openness, and to address some of those very motivation issues that may exist, your boss, Mike, has generously provided each of you with a copy of Contagious Confidence™. We'll start passing those out, and your first homework assignment will be to listen to those CDs and follow along with me as you start improving our own confidence to be who you are, really, so that you don't end up being that difficult person who is afraid to say you've got confidence and who forces someone else to break through that wall of protection you may have put up. That mountain will kill any motivation and stop all progress. Does that make sense?" The heads were nodding and looking around for the CD sets being passed out. It seemed as though this was the solution they had been looking for but were unable to articulate.

"We'll start passing those out, and raise your hand if you don't have one just yet."

The day had started without a hitch, and she knew already that lives would be transformed today, including her own.

The changes she had seen in Cybil had given her new insight into her work as well as a new perspective and a new attitude. In fact, it had been so powerful that she decided to share parts of it with her audience to show how the information they would cover today on the CORE Profile (the personalities, coaching, and recognition styles, the ways to be a better team member and create stronger results together) could be used in a way that felt effortless and produced immediate outcomes and massive motivation to make changes.

"While you are receiving your Contagious Confidence™ gift, and we're still handing those out, I also want to share with you something about one of my favorite students and coaching clients. In fact, I want to share with you the story of Cybil. . . ."

Today, as the trainer would with classes and audiences in her future, she would share how to make both her own difficult persona and those of the difficult people she had perceived to be around her, literally disappear. She would then focus on how, once the difficulty was gone, you could move mountains in motivating others.

For videos and more information that will enhance what you've learned in this chapter, go to: www.MakeDifficult PeopleDisappear.com.

The Disappearing Act

Whether you've been called a difficult person, think you are one, or have in fact been one at times, the question is, "Now what?" What's the next step, or maybe your next trick, in the seemingly magical mention of making difficult people disappear. Can you just make them vanish with a magic wand? Well, not exactly, but you *can* act on what you now know and the awareness you've gained about you and those around you. In fact, let's call it your very own Disappearing Act.

Here's what you'll need for your Disappearing Act:

- Compete the CORE Snapshot™ included in this book.

- Trust that *differences* do not equal *difficulties*.

- Fully understand your own behavioral description. Note: If you don't like your answers on the Snapshot™ or the behaviors they describe . . . change your answers.

- Examine which quadrant those who surround you might score the highest in, and remember that your perception is only a good guess. You may need more data.

- Give yourself permission to be who you are.

- Accept others for being who they are.

- Take notice of the times you become frustrated, and instead work toward being fascinated by the differences versus perceiving the frustration to be purposeful and aimed at you or able to affect you.

- Need more? Complete the comprehensive CORE Profile (www.ContagiousCoaching.com) and schedule a facilitation or coaching session by clicking "contact us" on the site. Often what you need is an outside point of view to determine the accuracy of what you're seeing inside of you.

The truth is, someone somewhere has likely called *you* difficult, and maybe they even told others or said it to your face, and that's okay. Either way, their perception and yours is real and right . . . for them. Right or wrong is not the question to be asked. Instead, look at whether you'd prefer to be right or successful. Your perceptions and those of others are always right, but the likelihood that they will create successful personal and professional relationships, work environments, or project outcomes is based on whether or not those perceptions are true and accurate.

To fortify your efforts in being *fascinated* instead of *frustrated*, ask yourself, "Is it true?" Ask yourself this question with regularity and then begin to look at the process of discovering much of what Cybil experienced. You could have a similar rapid transformation. You could have that happy ending. You can create your very own disappearing act.

People are not difficult by nature. They are often led astray by the voices in their head. Just as you hear yours and aren't sure which ones to pay attention to, the same is true for everyone else in your world. People do the best they can with what they know. Sometimes they simply don't do what works well for others, and our culture, unfortunately, often labels that behavior as wrong. It's not just that we think others are wrong or that what they do is wrong, but that repeated "wrongs" become annoying or harmful and that, when the person committing the "wrong" behavior doesn't change the way he or she does things (which, by the way, *works* for that person), the offender is labeled "difficult."

Difficult is a label. No more, no less. It serves the same purpose as wrong, but in this day and age, it has become the more commonly accepted standard by which we describe anyone whose behavior deviates repeatedly from the way we think it should be done. The problem is that, more often than not, once the label of "difficult" has been attached, it sticks . . . forever. Those who are so labeled are seen that way, no matter what they do, until you begin to see them differently.

That is a convoluted explanation of how people become known as difficult, but you've probably seen it happen in your office or personal life more than once. If you like being surrounded by difficult people or dealing with difficult people, don't change a thing. If, however, you would prefer things to be different, there are options available, such as you've just read about.

The CORE Profile is real. The training classes Cybil brought in are real, and so is the trainer. Contagious Companies has built a long-standing practice on transforming

189

Conclusion

managers who have been promoted but not prepared to lead into managers who are able to confidently lead employees who, in turn, stay longer, complain less, and produce more. They become more self-aware leaders able to lead themselves and thus to more effectively lead others. If you'd like to see your difficult people disappear, you and your organization can participate in a process just like the one you've read about here.

The truth is, it would be safe to say that difficult people, by and large, do not exist. Difficult behavior does. Stress-induced behavior and frustrated or mildly stressed reactions do exist. If you are faced with those behaviors, the CORE Profile and the self-awareness it provides is a solution. Through this tool, you, too, will learn to identify behaviors you've labeled as difficult, and you will understand where they come from. You will find out how your actions, labels, assumptions, and interactions create or dissipate difficult situations. You'll also be able to see immediately how these answers can be applied. If you find yourself in a pickle after following the seven steps and additional suggestions to *Make Difficult People Disappear*, and you're still frustrated, try simply saying "Cancel" until the frustration subsides. However, and this is important, say "Cancel" inside your head, not out loud. Others might really want to make you disappear if you look at a difficult person and say "Cancel" to his or her face. Though it's fun to think of how often you might be tempted to tell them that aloud.

Much of what we experience begins with the voices in our head, and sometimes we just need to tell them to hush. Maybe we should make the voices do a disappearing act all their own. That's what "Cancel" will help you with. However, the more long-term solution in your disappearing act is to raise your awareness of yourself and others and look at the unique contributions that come from the behavior of others.

Take an inventory of those you work with or live with or both. Assess how many times an inaccurate perception or lack of understanding has gotten in the way of high-functioning teamwork or stellar personal performance. Begin to ask yourself whether your perceptions are true. Move on to more productive thoughts if they're not, and then ask yourself what else can be done. Use "Cancel" if you're unable to overcome the emotion of the moment. Then take a closer look at what you expect from others. What do they expect from you? Are you leading and communicating in the way *you* like to be addressed, or in the way *they* need to hear it?

If you let go of the need for others to be difficult and conduct your own disappearing act, you can begin to accept not only yourself, but also others, who have their own differences and unique gifts, skills, and talents. With that, you may find you can get more done, but more important, you may find that we all need each other. You may find that we really can't do it on our own and need members of all personality preferences to carry out any given project or endeavor in life, successfully. In fact, if we stop focusing on wanting all those difficult people to disappear, we might discover how valuable they actually are in making us be even better.

Conclusion

Core Snapshot™

CORE Snapshot™
Page 1 of 2

Read each horizontal set of words and make one selection from either column A, B, C, or D. Select the one that , describes you most or most often. Once you have finished, record your total for each column. When added together, the totals should equal 18. If they do not, pleasecheck to be certain you have made a selection in each roooooowww, versus each column.

A	B	C	D
___Leader	___Planner	___Team Player	___Motivator
___Decisive	___Meticulous	___Flexible	___Enthusiastic
___Direct	___Technical	___Supportive	___Outgoing
___Problem Solver	___Structured	___Adaptable	___Energetic
___Driven	___Precise	___Sympathetic	___Spontaneous
___Goal Directed	___Scheduled	___Laid back	___Sociable
___Independent	___Sensible	___Compliant	___Imaginative
___Ambitious	___Organized	___Follows Rules	___Unpredictable
___Need a Challenge	___Need Order	___Need Stability	___Need Freedom
___Bold	___Careful	___Easygoing	___Persistent
___Action	___Logic	___Reassurance	___Excitement
___Take Charge	___Cautious	___Patient	___Approachable
___Impatient	___Perfectionistic	___Indecisive	___Forgetful
___Competitive	___Orderly	___Cooperative	___Convincing
___Self-directed	___Focused	___Extra-Miler	___People-oriented
___Restless	___Skeptical	___Undirected	___Undisciplined
___Influential	___Time Conscious	___Good Mediator	___Inspirational
___To the point	___Specific Details	___Helpful	___Interesting
_____Total	_____Total	_____Total	_____Total

The CORE Snapshot™ was designed to provide a quick look at your current self-perception. It is single dimensional and may or may not be an accurate representation of your true nature. Early conditioning or current circumstances may have altered your self-perception. An altered self-perception can result in lowered energy levels, inefficiency, discomfort with self and others, lack of focus or direction in life, increased stress levels, diminished health, and more. When you are not living authentically, true to your nature, life feels like a constant uphill battle. Discover your Authentic Self. For a complete and accurate picture of the entire spectrum of your personality, visit www.ContagiousCoaching.com.

COMMANDER (column A)	ORGANIZER (column B)
Normally:	**Normally:**
• Extroverted, Assertive, Serious	• Introverted, Reserved, Serious
• Thrives on Power and Authority	• Thrives on Order and Procedure
• Decisive – Results/Action Oriented	• Detailed – Systems Oriented
• Direct, Matter of Fact Relating	• Thorough, Cautious Relating
• Enjoys Competition, Challenge and Purposeful Activity	• Enjoys Structure, Predictability, and Factual Information
• Relates to Clear Cut Decisions and Tangible Benefits	• Relates to Constancy, Planning, Accuracy and Dependability
Under Stress Becomes:	**Under Stress Becomes:**
• Aggressive	• Passive Aggressive
• Bossy and Controlling	• Withdrawn/Cold
• Impatient	• Stubborn/Resistant
• Louder	• Narrow Minded
• Belligerent	• Silent or Sarcastic
ENTERTAINER (column D)	**RELATER (column C)**
Normally:	**Normally:**
• Extroverted, Assertive, Playful	• Introverted, Reserved, Playful
• Thrives on Action and Enthusiasm	• Thrives on Cooperation and Sharing
• Energetic – Interaction Oriented	• Patient – Construction Oriented
• Friendly, Matter of Fact Relating	• Friendly, Supportive Relating
• Enjoys Spontaneity, Change and Communicating	• Enjoys Stability, Reassurance, and Pleasant Surroundings
• Relates to Discussion, Debate, and Friendly Competition	• Relates to Loyalty, Flexibility, Consistency, and Duty
Under Stress Becomes:	**Under Stress Becomes:**
• Aggressive	• Passive, Submissive
• Pushy/Argumentative	• Withdrawn/Hurt
• Impatient	• Stubborn/Sensitive
• Louder	• Guilt Laden
• Demanding	• Silent or Tearful

About the Author

Monica Wofford, CSP, is the CEO of Contagious Companies, Inc., an Orlando-based training and consulting firm. Contagious Companies focuses on the development of confident leaders, with clients that have included Sea World, Olympus, Estée Lauder, the Federal Aviation Administration, and the Food and Drug Council. Monica is a business owner, an in-demand speaker, consultant, and coach specializing in providing training and consulting solutions that prevent managers from becoming those who have been promoted, but not prepared. Here proven techniques develop leaders who can coach, recognize and perform with repeatable real world strategies versus the typical managers' trial and error approach.

Monica has been called "that difficult person" at times. She's also a lifelong student of the methods used to minimize the application of this label and the behavior that provokes it. Her well-developed Commander preference is energized by multitasking and working long hours to help her clients develop into leaders who stay longer, produce more, and complain less. But it's her secondary Entertainer preference that induces folks to call her "Hilarious!" and

"Engaging!" and to accuse her of having had one too many Mountain Dews for breakfast.

Since her first keynote speech more than 20 years ago, she has worked with thousands to enhance their companies, careers, and lives. Her previous works include *Contagious Leadership* and *What Does Leadership Take?* As a Certified CORE Coach, her coaching clients have included many of the Who's Who of Corporate America. But, when she's not working, writing, or speaking, chances are you'll find Monica enjoying the Florida sunshine from the back of a galloping polo pony.

About the Author